# The Best
# 125 Meatless
# Pasta Dishes

If you have any feedback for us about this book, or if you would like to hear about our other offerings, please write to us in care of our publishers:

Mindy Toomay and Susann Geiskopf-Hadler
℅ Prima Publishing
P.O. Box 1260BK
Rocklin, CA 95677

Thanks for buying this book. We wish you great fun in the kitchen!

**How to Order:**

Quantity discounts are available from the publisher, Prima Publishing, P.O. Box 1260BK , Rocklin, CA 95677; telephone (916) 632-4400. On your letterhead include information concerning the intended use of the books and the number of books you wish to purchase.

# The Best 125 Meatless Pasta Dishes

**Mindy Toomay**
*and*
**Susann Geiskopf-Hadler**

**Prima Publishing**
P.O. Box 1260 BK
Rocklin, CA 95677
(916) 632-4400

PRIMA PUBLISHING and colophon are registered trademarks of Prima Communications, Inc.

Library of Congress Cataloging-in-Publication Data

Toomay, Mindy.
     The best 125 meatless pasta dishes / by Mindy Toomay
and Susann Geiskopf-Hadler.
          p.          cm.
     Includes index.
     ISBN 0-76150-645-4
     1. Cookery (Pasta). 2. Vegetarian Cookery. I. Geiskopf-
Hadler, Susann. II. Title. III. Title: Best one hundred
twenty-five meatless pasta dishes.  IV. Title: Best one hundred and twenty-five meatless pasta dishes.
     TX809.M17T59  1992                    91-31304
     641.8'22—dc20                              CIP

97 98 99 00 01 02 AA 10 9 8 7 6 5 4 3 2 1
Printed in the United States of America

How to Order
Single copies may be ordered from Prima Publishing, P.O.
Box 1260BK, Rocklin, CA 95677; telephone (916) 632-4400.
Quantity discounts are also available. On your letterhead,
include information concerning the intended use of the books
and the number of books you wish to purchase.

Visit us online at http://www.primapublishing.com

# Cook's Vow

Tomato, supple and serene,
offers itself to the sauce.
And just for a moment
I feel it. Surrender so deep:
full, ripe willingness
to transform.

I vow to work with the courage of flowers
opening,
as true to myself as an apple,
bright red.

Dusk paints its blush on my apron.
There are friends in the house
to be fed.

*Mindy Toomay*

# Acknowledgments

Everyone who helped to make me helped to make this book, and I appreciate you all. A very special thanks goes to my mother, the late Edith M. Cunningham Lackey, for being a wonderful model of creative cooking. Thank you to Lynn Hager, whose enthusiasm and expertise helped to fuel the first round of recipe production. Thanks to Ben Davis Jr., my way-back and still-going-strong vegetarian cooking comrade. And thanks especially to my neglected husband, Tad Toomay, and his sister Claire Toomay, long-suffering housemates who were forced to devour pound after pound of pasta during the development of this book. Indeed, thanks to the smiling parade of tasters that flowed through our house for months. You shall remain nameless here, but not forgotten (those who did dishes are sure to be richly rewarded in the afterlife). And a hearty thanks to the folks at Prima Publishing—particularly our editor, Jennifer Basye—for their energy, encouragement, and good cheer throughout the process. May we all continue to nourish each other.

*Mindy Toomay*

Fresh ingredients are inspiring and become the catalyst to creating delicious meals. My life is full of travel, which allows me to sample foods from many continents. I want to thank my mother, the late Jill Crampton Geiskopf, and my father, Earl Geiskopf, for instilling in me that sense of travel, and for giving me the confidence that I can succeed. Having an idea, then bringing it to life, is a wonderful accomplishment. I thank my husband, Guy Hadler, for growing so many vegetables and herbs for our table, and for being such an appreciative eater over the years. I would like to acknowledge Bunnie Day; she is a constant support person. I thank Lori Shull, my business associate, for running the business while I devoted my time to this book. My friend Linda Flamm, a self-proclaimed novice cook, helped to kitchen-test the recipes with very successful results! Thank you, Linda. Elizabeth Blaise has contributed creative ideas to the project, which have been well appreciated. To all of my dinner guests, thank you for eating and enjoying my creations. To the staff at Prima Publishing, and readers everywhere, I hope you enjoy creating these delicious, nutritious pasta recipes in your kitchen.

*Susann Geiskopf-Hadler*

# ✔ Almost Instant Recipes

*Almost Instant Recipes*

# Contents

✔ Almost Instant

# Tomato-Based Stovetop Sauces      **170**

# Dairy-Based Stovetop Sauces      **214**

## Baked and Stuffed Pasta                                257

# Cooking Up a Healthier Planet     296

# Index     303

# Introduction

Passion for pasta is an insatiable affair. To satisfy our hunger for simple, substantial nourishment, we turn again and again to pasta. How can a humble paste of flour and water inspire such devotion?

Perhaps we love it because it combines so deliciously with so many foods: mushrooms and garlic, vegetables and nuts, cheese and tomatoes, a gardenful of herbs. Whether hot or cold, whether sparsely or luxuriously dressed, the unpretentious character of pasta is endearing. What's more, most pasta dishes are quick and easy to prepare—they fit nicely into the puzzle of our busy lives. (Look for the Almost Instant designation on some recipes—they are particularly fast and easy to prepare.) Also to its credit, pasta is economical and nutritious. Health experts tell us to derive the greatest portion of our calories from complex carbohydrates, and pasta fills the bill. Those who have thought healthy food can't be delicious should reconsider.

Many pasta shapes and flavors inhabit this book, combined with a world of seasonings. Indian curry and the chilies of Mexico are as comfortable on a bed of noodles as the Sicilian olive is. So our out-of-the-ordinary dishes celebrate the cuisine of many nations, sometimes in unorthodox combinations.

Tradition has not been utterly abandoned. She hovers near the pantry, responding wisely to our queries but forbidden to meddle. Originality prevails in our kitchens—that is the fun and fulfillment of cooking!

# Putting Together Your Creative Pasta Kitchen

## A Well-Stocked Pasta Pantry

In addition to many shapes and sizes of dried pasta and an abundance of fresh vegetables, the well-stocked pasta kitchen contains a selection of the following essentials.

# Cooking Oils and Butter

The oil of choice for most pasta cooks is extra virgin olive oil. The pure essence of the olive, obtained from the fruit's initial pressing without the use of chemicals, it has a robust olive aroma and flavor that perfectly complement tomatoes, mushrooms, herbs, and other classic pasta partners. Extra virgin olive oil is flavorful enough to be a sauce unto itself, with few and simple additions like garlic, herbs, and cheese (for instance, Poppy Seed Noodles on page 129).

For certain purposes, low-calorie canola oil (also known as rapeseed oil) is a good substitute for olive oil. It tastes bland and unobtrusive, so it will not overpower a dish with an unwanted flavor. On the other hand, it won't contribute anything worthwhile to the flavor of a savory dish, as olive oil will. If you have fat-related health concerns, use canola oil when it seems appropriate. (Because of its blandness, we recommend you do not use canola oil in salad dressings.)

Other oils are occasionally preferred. In stir-frying ingredients for an Asian-style pasta, you may wish to use peanut oil, which tolerates high heat without smoking or burning. Also useful for Asian cooking and suggested in a few recipes in this book is roasted sesame oil, pressed from toasted sesame seeds. Its dark, smoky flavor is unique and quite delicious.

In some recipes, butter seems the natural choice. Cream sauces, for instance, usually begin with at least a little butter, and curry dishes traditionally use clarified butter rather than oil as a starting point. We prefer the unsalted variety for its purity and sweetness.

Those who count calories or cholesterol can usually reduce the amount of oil or butter called for in a recipe without disastrous results. Steaming onion, garlic, and spices in a few tablespoons of water before other ingredients are added is a fine alternative to the traditional oil or butter sauté, particularly in tomato-based and vegetable-based sauces.

*The Best 125 Meatless Pasta Dishes*

## Wines and Spirits

In moderation, fermented grape and grain beverages have a place in our diet. We find many culinary uses for certain types of alcohol, as well as enjoying wine as a refreshing libation with food.

In particular, you will note the use of port, sherry (both sweet and dry), and Madeira wines, and occasionally brandy, in our recipes. Mirin, a sweet rice wine from Asia, also makes several appearances. You can substitute sweet sherry if you don't have mirin on hand. The amounts used are not great, so the quantity of alcohol in each serving is negligible. The chemical composition of alcoholic beverages is altered by the cooking process, so foods containing them will not carry the alcohol bite some people find unpleasant.

Because the flavors of these wines and spirits are distinctive and essential to certain dishes, we suggest that those who object to their use simply bypass the recipes containing them.

## Tomatoes

Tomatoes in all their variety are important pasta partners. Keep canned whole tomatoes, tomato puree, stewed tomatoes, crushed tomatoes, and tomato paste on hand. They make fine sauces when good fresh tomatoes aren't available.

Dried tomatoes, now widely available, have inspired many a recipe in this book. When dried, tomatoes develop a chewiness and robust meaty flavor that is quite distinctive. Dried tomatoes can be purchased at some natural food markets in bulk or at well-stocked supermarkets in cellophane packages. They can also be found marinating in olive oil at your local Italian delicatessen. Marinated dried tomatoes can be costly, but a little goes a long way. Of course, the paper-dry variety can be stored in olive oil at home to achieve a texture similar to that of the gourmet Italian kind. Briefly immerse the dried tomatoes in boiling water, drain well, cover with extra virgin olive oil, and store in a closed container in the cupboard. The oil from the tomatoes can be used with delicious results in many recipes that call for olive oil.

Fresh tomatoes during their peak summer season make a light and flavorful pasta topping—whether cooked or raw—with the addition of only a few other ingredients. Grow your own in a pot on the porch if you have no garden plot, just to experience perfect tomato flavor and texture. Supermarket tomatoes take a poor second place in quality. If you must resort to marginally ripe supermarket tomatoes, buy them a couple of days in advance and ripen them in a basket at room temperature. Except when locally grown and purchased at the height of summer, tomatoes may not convey the characteristic sweetness prized by Italian cooks. Sometimes a little sugar is added to remedy this situation. Keep this in mind if the acidity of your tomato sauce needs a little mellowing.

## Garlic and Ginger

What can we say about garlic? You must love it to be considered a true pasta aficionado. Its pungent punch defines many classic pasta preparations. There are those who love pasta dressed only in a sprinkling of Parmesan cheese, perhaps a little fresh parsley, and a large quantity of minced garlic sautéed in butter or olive oil.

Fresh garlic is sold in bulbs, just as they come from the ground (though cleaned up a bit and with stalks removed). The bulb should be firm when you squeeze it. Garlic that is past its prime will dry and shrivel in the paper skin and you will notice this when you test the bulb. Store garlic bulbs in a dry, airy spot. Individual cloves are removed from the bulb, crushed gently with the side of a broad knife blade to separate the paper skin, and put through a press or finely minced with a sharp knife. As a rule of thumb, an average-size garlic clove yields about 1 teaspoon minced garlic.

Ginger, commonly used as a seasoning in Japanese and Chinese cuisine, appears in a few recipes in this book. You can purchase fresh ginger at any well-stocked supermarket. It is normally carried in large, many-lobed roots. Break off a smallish lobe and store it in a cool, dry place in the kitchen. When you are ready to use it, peel the root delicately with a paring knife and mince or grate it. A thick, juicy, aromatic pulp will result, which can be measured out. If the root dries up before you use it all, peel the shriveled root as well as you can and use your ginger grater to create a pungent fresh ginger powder. Store this in a dark, dry place and use it when a recipe calls for ground ginger.

Quantities of both garlic and ginger can be altered to suit your taste. In each recipe, we offer our recommendation as to what creates a well-balanced flavor, but your idea of well balanced may differ from ours. In all cases, with all seasonings, let your own experience and palate be your guide.


## Herbs and Spices

A cupboard well stocked with herbs and spices is a treasure trove for every cook. An amazing number of woody shrubs provide flavorful roots, leaves, stems, seeds, and flowers that not only season a dish but bolster its content of vitamins and minerals.

Of particular interest to pasta cooks—certainly to those with Italian leanings—are basil, oregano, rosemary, parsley, bay leaves, and nutmeg. Flat-leaf parsley, often referred to as Italian parsley, has a more distinctive flavor than the curly-leaf type. Dried red chili flakes are used in many of our recipes. Tarragon also makes several appearances. When stocking your herb shelf, be sure to include at least these basics.

Many dishes with Mexican and Chinese flavors call for fresh cilantro (also known as fresh coriander or Chinese parsley). If you particularly enjoy these types of cuisine, keep fresh cilantro on hand.

Freshly ground black pepper enlivens many of our favorite dishes. Invest in a simple pepper grinder and keep a supply of peppercorns on hand. Commercially packaged ground black pepper just isn't the same. Curry powder is a favorite seasoning of those who enjoy spicy cuisine. Different brands can vary vastly in potency, so discover one that suits your taste. Use curry (and all spicy seasonings) with discretion when guests are coming to dinner. Cayenne, the fiery red pepper of curry fame, provides an extra punch in certain strongly flavored dishes. Again, exercise caution.

An herb garden is one of the most satisfying projects creative cooks can undertake. In pots or in a spot of ground near your back door, plant seeds or set out seedlings purchased from a local nursery. Most herbs are easy to grow and quite hardy, so you needn't tend them much. Adequate water and sunlight are the only essentials for healthy and abundant herb plants. Some leafy herbs, such as basil and cilantro, are annuals and must be replanted each year. Woodier varieties—rosemary and oregano, for instance—will establish themselves readily in the right spot and will flourish for many, many years. You can easily dry fresh herbs from the garden by hanging them in a dark, dry place for several days.

If you don't wish to grow them yourself, you can buy fresh herbs at gourmet food stores or the larger supermarkets. Dried herbs in tins and jars are available at every grocery, but we suggest you seek out a source of bulk dried herbs—many natural food stores carry them. Then you can buy in small quantities at very reasonable prices. How many times have you paid two dollars or more for a fancy jar of spice, and never used more than a teaspoon or two? Store all dried herbs and spices covered in a dry, dark place to preserve freshness. Ground seasonings, in particular, lose their flavors rapidly.

*The Best 125 Meatless Pasta Dishes*

In most dishes, you can use either fresh or dried herbs. Pesto is an obvious exception—only fresh herbs will work. As a general rule of thumb, use twice as much of a fresh herb as you would dried. If a recipe calls for 1 teaspoon dried oregano, for instance, you can use 2 teaspoons minced fresh oregano with good results.

## Cheeses

We insist on natural cheeses, produced without added enzymes, gums, or preservatives. Become a label reader and select only real, pure cheese—avoid products labeled "processed" or "cheese food." Low-salt varieties may be easier on our blood pressure and are often just as flavorful as their salted counterparts. Many manufacturers are also offering skim-milk varieties. Some are quite tasty and can be substituted for their higher-fat counterparts in our recipes.

Dry, hard cheeses like Parmesan and Romano are high in fat and salt but impart a lot of flavor, even in small quantities. It's hard to imagine a pasta pantry without them. We buy these hard cheeses in wedges, grate them in sizable quantities, and store the grated cheese in the refrigerator in tightly closed containers (see Grinders and Graters on page 13). Parmesan, Romano, and Asiago can be used interchangeably in our recipes, with only slight variations in flavor.

Goat cheeses have a unique piquant flavor that some people adore; others find them too strong or "goaty." Feta, made from goat or sheep milk, must be stored in water in your refrigerator to retain its freshness. Other types of cheese should be tightly wrapped and stored in the refrigerator.

## Mushrooms

Because mushrooms are succulent and rich in flavor, they play an important role in many types of cuisine. Pasta is no exception. Many varieties of mushroom are available to today's cook, so you can experiment almost endlessly.

The fresh button mushroom most familiar to Americans is versatile and delicious. Choose button mushrooms that are an even white or light brown in color, with caps tightly closed against the stem. Store fresh button mushrooms in a dry paper or linen bag in the vegetable crisper of your refrigerator. They will retain optimum flavor and texture for only a few days, so buy in small quantities.

For a few dollars you can buy a mushroom brush, which is the perfect implement for removing loose dirt particles without damaging the mushroom's tender flesh. Brush the dirt from the mushrooms and slice off the often tough tip of the stem. Use them whole, halved, quartered, or sliced.

Also commonly available in their fresh form are shiitake—the rich, black mushroom of the Asian chef—and oyster mushrooms. Sometimes one can also find fresh cepes, chanterelles, morels, and other field mushrooms. All these varieties offer distinctive flavors and textures. Of course, there are many varieties of poisonous—even lethal—mushrooms, so don't pick the fresh fungus you find in your yard and throw it into the pot! It takes an experienced person to safely identify edible mushrooms.

Dried mushrooms further expand the variety of mushroom textures and flavors. Dried shiitake can be purchased in every Asian market. They are softened by soaking in water and are then carefully washed before using. Porcini, astoundingly robust Italian field mushrooms, are also soaked to reconstitute them before being added to a dish. In either case, strain the soaking liquid through a few layers of cheesecloth or a paper coffee filter and use it if liquid is called for in the recipe, or as a soup stock the following day. Porcini liquid compares to beef stock in its richness.

## Nuts and Seeds

Though nuts and seeds are high in fats—and therefore calories—they also provide amino acids, vitamins and minerals, and a great deal of flavor. Buy fresh, raw, unsalted nuts—in their shells when possible—and store in a cool, dry place. Once the shells are removed, the nuts should be stored in the refrigerator or freezer to avoid rancidity.

Seeds can also be purchased unsalted and raw—natural food stores often carry them in bulk. To protect their freshness, store seeds in tightly covered containers in a dark, dry cupboard or in the refrigerator.

Many of our recipes call for lightly toasted nuts or seeds. Toasting intensifies the natural flavors and imparts a pleasant subtle smokiness. (See page 20 for toasting instructions.)

Peanut butter and tahini (sesame paste) are examples of nut and seed preparations useful to the creative cook. Grind your own or purchase varieties that are made without additives and with little or no salt.

## Beans

Beans are wonderfully nutritious, delicious, and economical. Combined with pasta, they create a protein- and fiber-rich meal substantial enough to satisfy any appetite. Buy dried beans in bulk at a natural food store for the best variety and quality. Store them in tightly closed containers in a dark, dry place.

Before cooking beans, rinse them thoroughly to remove surface dirt, and sort them carefully. Often small dirt clods, pebbles, and other foreign objects will find their way through the factory sorters and into the market bean bin.

Most beans must be soaked several hours to soften them before cooking (overnight is fine, or all day if you put them to soak first thing in the morning). Drain off the starchy soaking liquid, which contributes to indigestion in some people. Cover the beans with fresh, cold water and boil them until they're tender. You may wish to add garlic, bay leaves, and/or dried red chili flakes to the cooking water, but wait to salt the pot until the beans are tender and ready for their final seasoning, because cooking in salt can give the beans a tough or rubbery texture.

When beans are to be added to another dish, as with the recipes in this book, be sure you do not let them get too soft in the boiling pot. Ideally, the beans will have a firm but delicate texture, yielding easily to the bite but not mushy.

## Tofu and Tempeh

Many vegetarians rely on tofu and tempeh, both derivatives of the soybean, as sources of concentrated protein. Tofu is made from soy milk curds and is available in a variety of textures, from silky smooth to coarse and firm. It tastes quite bland, and when added to pasta dishes will soak up the sauce and take on its flavor. Tofu can be sliced, diced, crumbled, or mashed. In every case, it is rinsed and blotted dry before using.

We often add tofu to ricotta cheese mixtures—in lasagna filling, for instance—because, when crumbled, its texture is similar. This increases the protein and calcium content of the dish and lowers the fat, without compromising the flavor.

Tempeh is a unique fermented soybean product with a chewy texture and authentic soybean flavor. It adds a hearty, even meaty, quality to certain dishes in this book.

Tofu and tempeh can be purchased at natural food stores and Asian specialty stores. In California, home to many health-conscious shoppers, tofu is available in the produce section of almost every supermarket. Tempeh, however, has yet to establish itself as a mainstream commodity. If you would like to be able to purchase tofu and tempeh at your local grocery, the manager may be willing to order it for you.

Fresh tofu keeps for a few days if stored in a bowl of water in the refrigerator. The water should be changed every day. You can also freeze tofu, though when frozen and thawed it takes on a spongy quality which will not lend itself to all tofu uses.

The refrigerator life of fresh tempeh is only a few days, so buy it just before you intend to use it, or freeze it if you wish to stock up. Tempeh freezes and thaws with no noticeable alteration in flavor or texture.

# Tools of the Craft

Artisans in every field will tell you that good tools are absolutely essential to creating fine things. Owning dishes and equipment of high quality will enhance your cooking experience considerably. There is great joy to be had in building piece by piece a beautiful and efficient cookware collection, whether at a gourmet kitchen shop or at flea markets and garage sales.

In writing this book, we have assumed that you are cooking in a kitchen well equipped with the basics. We offer the following suggestions regarding tools particular to pasta cooking. The essentials are few and simple.

## *Pasta Pot*

Any large stockpot can be used as your pasta-boiling kettle. It must hold a minimum of 8 quarts of water, and it should have a tight-fitting lid, because a closed pot will boil much more quickly than an open one. Since you will be using this vessel over high heat, select one with a heavy bottom that will conduct heat evenly and will not warp over time. You may want to purchase more than one, as such a pot will also be useful for cooking soups and blanching tomatoes.

## *Colanders*

The draining of pasta will soon become a frequent ritual, and the colander a valued utensil. Easy cleanup makes stainless steel colanders, which are sometimes coated with enamel, preferable. Obtain both a small one for intimate family use and a large one for grand affairs. Buy colanders with handles on both sides, since you will want to pick up the colander and shake it for really thorough draining. The footed type is ideal, since it holds the draining pasta a few inches away from the sink for maximum efficiency. If you choose to reuse pasta cooking water in the garden (but only if it isn't salted; see page 299), place the colander over a large basin or kettle to collect the liquid as it drains off.

## Pasta Machine

We have tried various types of pasta machines over the years, and keep coming back to the simplest: a heavy stainless steel, hand-cranked, countertop model that rolls the kneaded dough to the desired thickness and cuts it into uniform shapes. Though rolling pasta dough by hand and cutting it with a knife can work quite well, this device simplifies and expedites the process. The electric mix-and-extrude-type machine may work for you, but we prefer the more energy-efficient model for best hand-made results.

## Pasta Servers

Two specialized implements are available for serving pasta. Simple salad tongs—the stainless steel variety hinged together at the base—allow for efficient one-handed serving while the other hand holds the plate. Alternately, many people use a specialized gadget called a pasta claw, available in plastic, wood, or stainless steel. The noodles wrap around its stiff fingers and are then carried to the plate. Or you can simply use two wooden spoons, or a wooden fork and spoon, to lift the pasta from serving vessel to plate. For soups, of course, a ladle is the ideal serving implement. Acquire one with a large cup. Tongs, wooden implements, or steel-spring spoons are all useful tools for serving salad.

## Food Processor

There is certainly nothing absolutely essential about a food processor—unless you are a serious cook! The vast capabilities of these devices open up new worlds of culinary possibility. For certain jobs, like pesto making, cheese grating, or fine mincing of ingredients, the time saved by a food processor is considerable. A blender can come in handy for some simple blending jobs, but invest in a real food processor as soon as you can. Today, small-capacity machines are available, which can serve most purposes for a fraction of the cost of the larger models.

## Grinders and Graters

Canned ground spices bear very little resemblance to the aromatic powder that results when you grind whole spices as you need them. Noteworthy examples are black pepper, cloves, nutmeg, and mustard. You may wish to purchase a small electric coffee grinder to use only for spices (be sure to label it prominently so some unintiated soul doesn't use it for coffee!). For similar results, you can obtain a mortar and pestle—a sharply ridged bowl with pounding stick—and engage in the ancient cooking ritual of manually breaking up spices to release their flavors. Specialized grinders are available for black pepper and whole nutmeg. They are worth the investment. Spices and herbs are the cook's inspiration—make the most of them by preparing them fresh.

   Graters come in a wide variety of shapes and sizes. The standard flat grater or the four-sided stand-up model are both quite adequate for most tasks. We both own tripod hand-crank disc graters and rely on them for large grating jobs. These wonderful little machines come with different sizes of grating and slicing discs, and yours will soon become indispensable. For grating hard cheeses like Parmesan, a food processor will save you time and effort.

# Perfect Pasta Every Time

## Selecting the Noodle

Fresh pasta or dried? What a happy choice! Either way, you can dazzle family and friends with your delicious sauce inventions.

Some cooks have a strong preference for fresh pasta. Newly made noodles can have a delightfully delicate texture and a bright, fresh taste. Also, consider the simple pleasure to be had in preparing food from scratch. If you enjoy being industrious in your kitchen, creating fresh pasta may become a favorite pastime. There is an art to pasta-making. If the dough is kneaded too little or too much, you may end up with pasta that is rubbery or limp. Attention to the task can avert these disasters, however, so please don't hesitate to give it a try.

At fine gourmet food stores, commercially prepared fresh noodles come in a variety of herb and vegetable flavors not commonly available dried. Be aware of dates on the packaging, though. Fresh pasta that sits too long at the market develops an off flavor that no sauce, however inspired, can mask. Select fresh noodles that are no more than a day (perhaps two) old.

Some cooks greatly prefer dried pasta, not only for its convenience but because the hard semolina wheat used by most commercial pasta manufacturers ensures real body to the pasta (so long as it's not overcooked!). We find that dried semolina pasta is delicious for most purposes. Locate an Italian deli-type market in your community for the largest selection of shapes and sizes.

Many of our recipes suggest using Asian noodle varieties. Many well-stocked supermarkets sell fresh Chinese noodles and wonton wrappers, which are delicious. You might be able to seek out buckwheat, rice, or yam flours to make your own Asian noodles from scratch, but we find the dried noodles sold in great variety at specialty food markets to be quite fine.

Couscous is a pasta import from North Africa. The tiny beads of dried flour and water cook almost instantly, creating a light and fluffy texture perfect for salads and casseroles. Couscous is available at any well-stocked supermarket.

In summary, with so many good dried and fresh noodles available in Italian and Asian food stores—and even standard supermarkets—there's no need to invest the time required to make your own. But it's fun now and then to begin at the beginning if you have plenty of time and want to experience the joys of "from scratch" cooking. The recipes in this book are written primarily for dried noodles, but you may substitute the fresh variety. One pound dried pasta is equivalent to 1½ pounds fresh, so convert the recommended amounts and you will be sure to prepare enough.

With this in mind, we provide here a basic and relatively simple egg pasta recipe. In addition to the right ingredients, all you need is a large work surface, a rolling pin, and a knife or scissors for cutting the shapes. If you find you love it and want to enjoy fresh pasta more than occasionally, consider investing in a hand-crank pasta machine, which will roll the dough out to a uniform thickness and will cut strands of varying widths quickly and easily.

# Basic Egg Noodles

*Yield:* 1½ pounds (enough for about 4 servings)

| | | |
|---|---|---|
| White all-purpose flour | 1¾ | cup |
| Semolina flour | ½ | cup |
| Salt | ½ | teaspoon |
| Eggs | 3 | large, room temperature |
| Olive oil | 1 | tablespoon |
| Water | 3 | tablespoons |

Place flours and salt in the work bowl of a food processor and process briefly to combine. With machine running, add eggs, oil, and water and process until dough resembles coarse cornmeal and sticks together when pressed between thumb and forefinger. If you don't own a food processor, stir together the flours and salt and pour into a compact mound on your work surface. Make a well in the center of the mound and pour in the slightly beaten eggs, oil, and water. Stir with a fork, incorporating the flour a little at a time, until you have a smooth dough.

Wrap the dough in a floured tea towel and set aside at room temperature for about 30 minutes. Knead gently about 10 times, then roll out with a rolling pin to desired thickness and cut into shapes. You may also use a hand-crank pasta machine for these steps, following manufacturer's directions. If preparing in advance, spread pasta out on a floured tea towel, dust with a little flour, and toss occasionally until you are ready for it. Pasta can also be left to dry on the towel, or on a rack, for longer periods. When it is completely dry, store it in a sealed container in a dark, dry place until needed.

*Variations:* A lovely green pasta will result if you substitute ¼ pound fresh pureed spinach for one of the eggs. For herb-flecked pasta, add ¼ cup minced fresh basil or ½ cup minced fresh tarragon to the flour mixture. Wonderful pasta can be made using minced dried tomatoes or chilies, or any number of other ingredients. Experiment and see what flavor discoveries you can make on your own.

---

Each serving provides:

| | | | |
|---|---|---|---|
| 339 | Calories | 53 g | Carbohydrate |
| 12 g | Protein | 322 mg | Sodium |
| 8 g | Fat | 159 mg | Cholesterol |

---

## Perfecting the Noodle

"He can't even boil water!" So complained a close friend about her kitchen-phobic husband. Well, he might have trouble becoming a pasta chef. But anyone who's mastered the boiling of water can easily learn to delight family and friends with delicious pasta.

A great pasta dinner depends on a well-cooked noodle, so the boiling part is important. To begin with, use plenty of water: 8 quarts per pound of pasta is about right. Bring it to a real rolling boil (a lid on the pot helps this happen faster) before adding a bit of olive oil and a shake or two of salt. Those with fat- or salt-related health concerns can skip these ingredients, but they are part of the time-tested method for a successful batch of noodles.

Add the pasta all at once to the boiling water, separating the strands a little as you immerse them. Now, stay close to the pot! Stir the noodles regularly to see that they aren't sticking together or to the pan. If you are still in the middle of preparing the sauce or some other part of the meal, set a timer to alert you when the pasta cooking time is almost up. If you are using store-bought dried noodles, the package will give you the approximate cooking time. Set your timer for just a couple of minutes less than is recommended so you can pull out a noodle and bite into it to test for doneness.

Most pasta chefs prefer their noodles cooked to the "al dente" stage. This Italian phrase means "to the tooth" and suggests that the tooth should meet a little resistance in the pasta. Undercooked pasta has a tough center and an unpleasant starchy taste. Cooked too long, noodles break apart easily and turn to mush in the mouth. You must learn to get it right! If you are calmly attentive the first few times you try, soon it will become second nature to recognize perfectly cooked noodles.

Fresh noodles, whether homemade or store-bought, cook very rapidly—in only a minute or two, depending on their shape and texture. When cooking fresh pasta, don't leave the pot even for a moment! Stir the noodles in, watch as the water comes back to a boil, then immediately pull out a noodle and bite into it. If it's not yet al dente it soon will be, so stay and check again half a minute or so later.

We would recommend one exception to the al dente rule: Some Asian noodles, particularly soba (made with buckwheat flour) and rice flour noodles, taste better if they are cooked to the soft stage. Not mushy, but a bit beyond al dente.

When the pasta is cooked to perfection, drain it quickly in a large colander, allowing just a little water to cling to each noodle (unless a recipe stipulates thorough draining). Toss the pasta and sauce together in a serving dish. A warmed platter or bowl is preferable, as most pasta dishes are at their best served really hot. A serving bowl can be warmed briefly atop your boiling pasta pot, or use the oven or a warm spot on your stovetop.

It works best to have the sauce ready when the noodles come out of the pot, but timing is not always perfect. If you must hold the noodles for a few minutes, toss them with a little butter or olive oil in the still warm but dry boiling pot and keep a lid on until you're ready for them. Or, if you know ahead of time that the sauce is going to take a bit longer, stop the pasta water from boiling and let the noodles simply rest in the hot water while the sauce catches up. But pay attention! Though it cooks more slowly once the burner is turned off, the pasta will get overly soft if left in the water too long. This method is for the rare emergency when the sauce is running only a few minutes behind.

There may come a time when you will need to hold the cooked, unsauced pasta a long while before serving. Or you may have leftover plain pasta to heat up. When this happens, boil a pot of water and stir the noodles in for about 30 seconds just before tossing with the sauce. If a finished pasta gets gooey from sitting too long before serving, incorporate hot water a drizzle at a time to correct the consistency.

If you're making pasta salad, cool the noodles by plunging them into a bowl of cold water for 2 to 3 minutes (this is preferable to the running-faucet cooling method because it conserves water). If your salad dressing isn't ready yet, toss the noodles with a little olive oil and set aside in the refrigerator.

Some people like a greater ratio of sauce to noodle; adjust the recommended amount of pasta to suit your taste. Learn to trust yourself more than even the most famous cookbook authors.

Pasta cooking can be a wonderfully relaxing and creative experience. The basics are easy to learn. Use high-quality ingredients, and have fun in the kitchen!

# The Basics of Sauce

As we have said elsewhere, the fun of cooking is in experimentation. This makes pasta one of the cook's most enjoyable foods, because the possibilities for sauce are practically limitless. Within each category, we provide numerous examples of how we combine our favorite foods with pasta. We invite you to take off from there.

In an introduction to each recipe section, we have provided tips and techniques for successful sauce preparation. Please read those introductions for a comprehensive overview.

Here, we explain some basic flavor-enhancing techniques used in various recipes in this book. They are simple and quick procedures. Once you have mastered them, you will find them quite useful.

## Toasting Seeds and Nuts

Place nuts or seeds in a single layer in a heavy-bottomed skillet over medium-high heat on the stovetop. Shake the pan frequently and soon the nuts or seeds will be golden brown and will emit a wonderful roasted aroma. Whole spices, like mustard or cumin seeds, are done when they begin to pop vigorously in the pan. Remove immediately from the pan and set aside until needed.

## Blanching and Seeding Tomatoes

Bring several quarts of water to a boil in a large lidded pot (the same water can be used later for cooking pasta). Drop in the fresh tomatoes. Within a minute or two, their skins will begin to split and pull away from the flesh. Remove with a slotted spoon to a bowl of cold water. When they are cool enough to handle, remove the skins of the tomatoes and cut out the stems. If you are using pear tomatoes (also known as plum tomatoes), they can be coarsely chopped and used without further preparation. If using the rounder salad type, cut the peeled tomatoes in half crosswise and gently squeeze to remove the juicy seed pockets. Now chop the tomatoes coarsely and proceed with the recipe.

## Roasting Vegetables

Certain vegetables take on a delightful smoky flavor when roasted. Peppers and small eggplants lend themselves most readily to this type of preparation. Place the vegetable under a very hot broiler and turn every few minutes until the entire surface is charred black. Remove it to a paper or plastic bag, close, and set aside for about 15 minutes. The steam in the bag will finish the cooking and the vegetable will become quite soft. When cool enough to handle, remove it from the bag and peel off the charred skin. Remove stems and/or seeds and chop or mash before proceeding with the recipe.

# Nutrition Alert

People who are concerned about nutrition balance their food intake based on factors beyond the outmoded "five basic food groups" concept. Some of us do this because of a health condition that requires special attention; others simply want to maintain the best health possible.

Many studies have been conducted to determine optimum levels of various food components in the human diet. Our intent here is to suggest some guidelines based on the latest findings. For further investigation, check with your local librarian or bookseller.

Each recipe in this book has been analyzed for calories, fats, proteins, carbohydrates, cholesterol, and sodium.

**Calories.** Almost everyone is concerned about calories—either with ingesting too many or, rarely, too few. It is important to be aware of your total caloric intake in a day, but most important to note is where the calories are coming from. Calories derive from three primary sources: proteins, carbohydrates, and fats. Fats contain a greater concentration of calories than do carbohydrates or protein, and they are much harder for the body to metabolize. Government dietary experts suggest that the average American diet be adjusted so that fewer calories come from fatty foods and more from carbohydrates. Pasta fits nicely into this picture, providing a good carbohydrate foundation for a meal.

**Fats.** In the nutritional analyses provided here, fat is listed in grams per serving. A gram of fat has 9 calories. The average tablespoon of oil contains 125 calories. To help you put this in perspective, consider that a tablespoon of sugar contains 54 calories. Calories derived from dietary fats are more troublesome than calories from any other source, as the body is most efficient at converting fat calories into body fat. The American Heart Association recommends limiting fat intake to no more than 30 percent of total calories.

Although sophisticated nutritional studies have broken fats into three classifications—saturated, monounsaturated, and polyunsaturated—the recipes in this book have been analyzed for overall fat content, to offer a basic guideline for monitoring dietary fat intake.

**Proteins.** Protein is also analyzed in this book for grams per serving. Each gram of protein contains only 4 calories. Since our bodies store only small amounts of protein, it needs to be replenished on a daily basis. Most people associate protein consumption with eating animal products; however, protein in our recipes derives from combining grains (pasta flour) with soy products, dairy products, beans, and nuts. Readers who are not vegetarians may wish to serve a pasta dish as an accompaniment to meat or fish, keeping overall protein (and fat) intake in mind. Recent nutritional studies suggest that the detrimental effects of excessive protein consumption should be of greater concern to most Americans than the threat of protein deficiency.

**Carbohydrates.**    Carbohydrates are analyzed here for grams per serving. Each carbohydrate gram provides 4 calories, equivalent to proteins. Carbohydrates such as pasta, grains, and potatoes were once thought to be high in calories and low in nutritive value. However, nutritional experts now suggest that more of our daily calories come from carbohydrates and fewer from protein, since the body derives energy more "economically" from carbohydrates.

**Cholesterol.**    Cholesterol content is listed in milligrams for our recipes. Many volumes have been written on this subject in recent years, and much is being discovered about its role in overall health and nutrition. Accumulation of cholesterol in the cells lining our artery walls can lead to atherosclerosis, heart attacks, and strokes. More crucial to the health of your blood vessels than cholesterol count, however, is the amount of total dietary fats you ingest.

**Sodium.**    Sodium content of our recipes is listed in milligrams. The American Heart Association recommends that sodium intake be limited to 3,000 milligrams a day (a teaspoon of salt contains 2,300 milligrams of sodium). High sodium intake is associated with high blood pressure and such life-threatening conditions as heart and kidney diseases and strokes. Many foods naturally contain some sodium, so you do not need to add much when cooking to achieve good flavors. Particularly if you have salt-related health concerns, dishes that taste a little bland unsalted can be seasoned with herbs or other salt-free alternatives. Where our recipes do call for salt, you may add less than the recommended amount or none at all, if you wish.

Monitoring your intake of these food components is important; however, unless under doctor's instructions, you needn't be overly rigid. It is acceptable to balance your intake over the course of a day, rather than attempting to make each meal fit the pattern recommended by nutritional experts. This rule of thumb allows you to enjoy a recipe that may be higher in fat or salt, for instance, than you would normally choose, knowing that at your next meal you can eliminate that component altogether to achieve a healthy daily balance.

The information given here is not set in stone; the science of nutrition is constantly evolving. We encourage you to spend some time learning about how foods break down and are used by the body as fuel. A basic understanding of the process and application of a few simple rules can contribute to a longer and—more important—healthier life.

# An Introduction to the Recipes

Before you try our recipes, we want to outline some basic information that we hope will make using them an experience of great pleasure.

There are a few standard rules for preparing to cook from a recipe.

1. Use only the freshest, best-quality ingredients. Your finished dish will be only as good as the individual components that go into it, so don't compromise on quality. (We've said this before, but it bears repeating.)

2. Read the recipe all the way through before beginning. This will give you a solid understanding of the entire process so you can proceed with confidence. You wouldn't think of building a house without first having studied the blueprints!

3. Set all of your ingredients out on the work surface before you begin. This will save you walking from one end of the kitchen to the other to rummage in a cupboard for the long-lost paprika, while your vegetables are overcooking on the stove.

4. For certain ingredients, quantities are by nature somewhat approximate. When we call for a large carrot, for instance, the one you use may be more or less large than ours. This is nothing to worry about. When it is essential to the success of a dish to use a very specific amount, we will provide cup or pound measurements. Otherwise, use your own judgment in deciding which carrot in the bin is "large." Our method with garlic deserves special mention here. We have listed garlic amounts in "medium" cloves. If you are using elephant garlic, or the tiny new cloves at the center of a garlic bulb, adjust accordingly the number of cloves you use.

5. Seasonings are a matter of personal taste. Naturally, we have provided recipes for dishes that taste good to us, seasoned as we like them. Certain people will prefer more or less of certain seasonings: salt and garlic are prominent examples. Of course, you may do as you please. We often customize favorite recipes from cookbooks, and we encourage you to do the same.

6. When serving hot food, use warmed serving dishes and warmed plates so the food stays at optimum temperature as long as possible. This is easily accomplished by placing the dishes near the heat source as you cook; or warm your oven several minutes before dinnertime, turn off the heat, and place your dishes there until needed.

You will notice that our recipes list ingredients in an unconventional format: name of food in first column, quantity required in a separate column to the right. This allows the quickest perusal of the ingredients, so you can determine whether you're in the mood for that particular dish, and whether you have the required foods on hand. We find this format particularly easy to follow, and hope you will agree.

Some recipes in this book carry an "Almost Instant" designation. This means that you can prepare the sauce in the time it takes to boil water and cook the pasta. When time is short, check for "Almost Instant" dishes in the recipe lists under chapter headings in the table of contents. Put the pasta water on and you're almost there!

Now, we invite you to enjoy our favorite pasta dishes.

# Pestos

The word *pesto* literally means "paste." The fresh basil version is an Italian classic and now a common American restaurant and supermarket offering; many other foods lend themselves to this type of preparation as well. Once you are accustomed to the basic technique, experiment and enjoy!

The classic pesto ingredients are fresh herbs, nuts, cheese, and garlic—with an emphasis on the garlic. For many, in fact, eating pesto is a fine way to achieve garlic bliss. Some of the recipes in this section suggest using just a clove or two so the more subtle flavors aren't lost. You may use whatever amount of garlic suits your taste, of course.

A revelation of freshness, most pesto is uncooked and quick to prepare. Once the raw ingredients are readied for blending, you're only a few minutes away from serving time. Before the age of electricity, cooks used a mortar and pestle to pound their ingredients into a thick mush. Today, a food processor saves a great deal of time and effort. A blender can also do the job, though not as efficiently.

High-quality ingredients are essential to great pesto. Make sure greens and herbs are crisply fresh, and dry them well before blending (a salad spinner works well for this). You want a finished product that is wonderfully thick, not watery. Shell the nuts immediately before using (except in the case of pine nuts, which are difficult to find in their natural state). Nuts sold already shelled are often rancid in the package and will ruin your pesto. Use the finest-quality cheeses and the best olive oil—extra virgin—because its authentic olive flavor pulls the other tastes together.

Pesto improves over time as the flavors blend. For this reason, we prefer preparing pesto ahead of time and storing it, covered, in the refrigerator at least several hours before using. The basic herbal pestos will keep in the refrigerator several weeks, while the more exotic pestos should be used within a few days. Many pestos can also be made in large quantities and frozen in small jars until needed. But don't try it with those that contain high-water-content dairy products (sour cream, for instance). These milk products may separate when thawed and ruin the consistency of your pesto. Hard, dry cheeses like Parmesan are an exception to this rule.

If you are using pesto that has been frozen or refrigerated, bring it to room temperature before using it. A cold pesto will cool your noodles too rapidly. Also, the cooked pasta should be really hot when you add the pesto, so the thick sauce will be liquefied a bit and will coat the noodles well.

Don't overlook the many other uses for pesto. We enjoy it as a sandwich or cracker spread, either plain or in combination with cream cheese. It can also be used in soups, salad dressings, and as a stuffing seasoning.

Pasta al pesto is at once simple and sophisticated. If you are not yet a devoted pesto lover, the following recipes will make one of you.

## Basic Herbal Pestos

Your favorite herbs can be easily transformed into flavorful pastes for pasta saucing, and other uses. The basic herbal pastes discussed here are called for as flavoring agents in a number of recipes throughout this book. Grow your own herbs, if you can, and stock up on a variety of pestos. You will discover many creative ways to enjoy them.

To whip up a quick and delicious meal, heat several quarts of water and boil pasta until al dente. Drain and toss with enough pesto to coat the noodles well. (As a rule of thumb, use 1 cup pesto for 1 pound pasta.) Add additional cheese if desired.

The strong, woody flavors of rosemary and oregano may not appeal in concentrated form to all palates, so experiment to see what you like.

# Classic Basil Pesto

*We have both prepared this simple version of the classic Genovese pesto for years, using aromatic basil picked fresh from the summer garden. It is satisfying work which will bring you and your friends great pleasure at the table.*

*Yield:* 1 cup

| | | |
|---|---|---|
| **Fresh basil leaves** | **2** | **cups, firmly packed** |
| **Olive oil** | **⅓** | **cup** |
| **Pine nuts** | **¼** | **cup** |
| **Garlic** | **6** | **medium cloves, chopped** |
| **Parmesan cheese, finely grated** | **¾** | **cup** |

Wash the basil, discard the stems, and spin dry. In a food processor or blender puree basil with ¼ cup of the olive oil, the pine nuts, garlic, and Parmesan until thick and homogenous. With the machine running, add the remaining olive oil in a thin stream to form a smooth paste.

*Note:* If you are harvesting basil from the garden at season's end, a few simple tips will facilitate cleaning of the leaves. Use your clippers to snip off the main stems near the base of the plant, rather than pulling them up by the roots. Put a spray attachment on your hose and wash down the plants before bringing them into the kitchen.

---

Each serving (1 tablespoon) provides:

| | | | |
|---|---|---|---|
| 85 | Calories | 4 g | Carbohydrate |
| 3 g | Protein | 87 mg | Sodium |
| 7 g | Fat | 4 mg | Cholesterol |

---

*The Best 125 Meatless Pasta Dishes*

# Rosemary Pesto

*Rosemary is a strong-flavored herb that makes an exciting and unusual pesto. A flat-leaf variety can be grown in home gardens. It is more fragrant and finer in texture than the more common woody type. Either will work, but remember, a little goes a long way. To create a sauce for 8 ounces of noodles, whip ⅓ cup pesto with about ¼ cup half-and-half or light sour cream. Toss with hot pasta and enjoy.*

*Yield:* 1⅓ cups

| | | |
|---|---|---|
| **Fresh parsley** | 1½ | cups, firmly packed |
| **Fresh rosemary leaves** | ½ | cup, loosely packed |
| **Garlic** | 6 | medium cloves, chopped |
| **Olive oil** | ½ | cup |
| **Parmesan cheese, finely grated** | ½ | cup |
| **Dried red chili flakes** | ¼ | teaspoon |
| **Raw walnuts, chopped** | ¼ | cup |

Wash the parsley and rosemary, discard stems, and spin dry. In a food processor or blender puree herbs, garlic, and ¼ cup of the olive oil until thick and homogenous. Add the Parmesan, chili flakes, and walnuts, and blend again. With the machine running, add the remaining olive oil in a thin stream. A thick, rich paste will result.

---

### Each serving (1 tablespoon) provides:

| | | | |
|---|---|---|---|
| 93 | Calories | 2 g | Carbohydrate |
| 2 g | Protein | 60 mg | Sodium |
| 9 g | Fat | 2 mg | Cholesterol |

---

# Cilantro Pesto

*Of course, you must be a cilantro fan to enjoy the flavor of this pesto. We love it simply spread on crackers with cream cheese. Or use it to season south-of-the-border pasta dishes, such as Pasta with Cilantro Pesto and Avocado, page 135. The roasted garlic called for in this recipe imparts a mellower, sweeter flavor than raw minced garlic.*

*Yield:* 1 cup

| | |
|---|---|
| Garlic | 1 large bulb |
| Pumpkin seeds | ⅓ cup |
| Fresh cilantro | 1 cup, firmly packed |
| Fresh parsley | 1 cup, firmly packed |
| Olive oil | ⅓ cup |
| Mild chili powder | 2 teaspoons |
| Dried red chili flakes | 1 teaspoon |
| Ground cumin | 1 teaspoon |
| Lemon juice | ¼ cup |

Preheat oven or toaster oven to 350 degrees. Cut ¼ inch off the garlic bulb to barely expose the tops of the cloves. Do not peel. Drizzle on about ½ teaspoon olive oil and bake about 30–45 minutes. Alternately, bake in a microwave oven until soft, about 15 minutes. When the garlic bulb is very soft, remove it from the oven and cool. Remove the garlic from the skin by squeezing the cloves from the bottom. The garlic will slide out of the cut end as a soft paste. Toast the pumpkin seeds (see page 20).

Wash the cilantro and parsley, discard stems, and spin dry. In a food processor or blender, combine the cilantro, parsley, and olive oil. Puree into a thick paste. Add the garlic, toasted pumpkin seeds, chili powder, chili flakes, cumin, and lemon juice. Puree until smooth.

---

Each serving (1 tablespoon) provides:

| 38 | Calories | 2 g | Carbohydrate |
|---|---|---|---|
| 0 g | Protein | 5 mg | Sodium |
| 3 g | Fat | 0 mg | Cholesterol |

---

# Oregano Pesto

*Oregano pesto is more delicate in flavor than many other herbal pestos. The herb is a perennial, so grow it in a large pot or on a small spot of unused ground to harvest year-round.*

*Yield:* 1 cup

| | | |
|---|---|---|
| **Fresh parsley** | 1½ | **cups, firmly packed** |
| **Fresh oregano leaves** | ½ | **cup, firmly packed** |
| **Olive oil** | ½ | **cup** |
| **Pine nuts** | ¼ | **cup** |
| **Garlic** | 4 | **medium cloves, chopped** |
| **Parmesan cheese, finely grated** | ½ | **cup** |
| **Port** | 2 | **teaspoons** |

Wash the parsley and oregano, discard stems, and spin dry. Combine parsley, oregano, and ¼ cup of the olive oil in a food processor or blender. Process briefly to chop the herbs. Add the pine nuts, garlic, and Parmesan. With the machine running, add the remaining oil in a thin stream, and the port. Process into a smooth paste.

---

### Each serving (1 tablespoon) provides:

| | | | |
|---|---|---|---|
| 94 | Calories | 2 g | Carbohydrate |
| 2 g | Protein | 60 mg | Sodium |
| 9 g | Fat | 2 mg | Cholesterol |

---

# Pesto Exotica

Many foods are perfect fodder for pesto. Your favorite combinations of flavors can easily be translated into delicious thick paste concoctions for pasta. Below are some of the near-infinite possibilities.

We include the amount of dried pasta recommended for a full recipe of pesto, as well as the number of servings provided by these amounts. We hope this will suggest to you that pesto is wonderful dinner party fare. If you are serving fewer people, simply reduce the amount of pasta accordingly and save the pesto that isn't used for another time. As a rule of thumb for moderate appetites, plan on 2 ounces of pasta per person for pesto side-dish servings and 3 ounces per person for pesto main-course servings.

# Pimiento Olive Pesto

*The sharp flavor of pimiento-stuffed olives is mellowed here by the other ingredients. In fact, most people will not guess the primary ingredient of this pesto, though they will eat it in large quantities.*

*Yield:* 8 main-course servings

| | | |
|---|---|---|
| Pimiento-stuffed olives, drained | 1 | cup |
| Raw walnuts, chopped | ½ | cup |
| Olive oil | ¼ | cup |
| Madeira | ¼ | cup |
| Parmesan cheese, finely grated | ¼ | cup |
| Fresh parsley, chopped | ¼ | cup, firmly packed |
| Garlic | 2 | medium cloves, chopped |
| Pepper | | Several grinds |
| Dried pasta | 1½ | pounds |

*Recommended pasta:* lasagnette or linguine

Puree all ingredients except pasta in a food processor or blender until a thick, color-flecked paste is formed. Prepare this pesto well ahead of time, if possible, so the flavors have time to blend. Store covered in the refrigerator. When ready to eat, put several quarts of water on to boil and bring the pesto to room temperature. Cook pasta in boiling water until al dente.

*The Best 125 Meatless Pasta Dishes*

Toss the pesto with hot noodles in a warm bowl until well distributed. Pass more cheese and the pepper grinder, if you wish.

| | Each serving provides: | | |
|---|---|---|---|
| 471 | Calories | 67 g | Carbohydrate |
| 14 g | Protein | 473 mg | Sodium |
| 16 g | Fat | 2 mg | Cholesterol |

# Black Olive and Tomato Pesto

*This tantalizing pesto is a quickie to prepare. The calamata or Greek olives add special pizzazz. A tart salad or a platter of crisp, raw bell pepper strips and garlic bread would be most welcome on the side.*

*Yield:* 8 main-course servings

| | | |
|---|---|---|
| **Pitted black olives, drained** | 1½ | **cups** |
| **Calamata or Greek olives, chopped** | ¼ | **cup, firmly packed** |
| **Olive oil** | 2 | **tablespoons** |
| **Tomato paste** | ⅓ | **cup** |
| **Dried oregano** | 1 | **teaspoon** |
| **Garlic** | 4 | **medium cloves, minced** |
| **Pepper** | | **A few grinds** |
| **Parmesan cheese, finely grated** | ⅔ | **cup** |
| **Dried pasta** | 1½ | **pounds** |

*Recommended pasta:* **vermicelli or linguine**

Put several quarts of water on to boil for the pasta. Drain the olives and puree them with the oil, tomato paste, oregano, garlic, pepper, and ⅓ cup of the Parmesan in a food processor or blender to a thick, homogenous paste consistency. Cook the pasta until al dente and drain well. Toss in a warm bowl with the pesto. Serve immediately, passing additional Parmesan.

---

Each serving provides:

| | | | |
|---|---|---|---|
| 127 | Calories | 5 g | Carbohydrate |
| 4 g | Protein | 642 mg | Sodium |
| 11 g | Fat | 6 mg | Cholesterol |

---

# Roasted Red Bell Pepper Pesto

*This makes a beautiful pale pink pesto which is lovely on a green noodle. Either home-roasted (see page 21) or commercially prepared peppers will do for this dish.*

*Yield:* 8 main-course servings

| | | |
|---|---|---|
| **Roasted red bell peppers** | 1 | **cup, loosely packed** |
| **Part-skim ricotta cheese** | ½ | **cup** |
| **Olive oil** | ¼ | **cup** |
| **Capers, drained** | 2 | **tablespoons** |
| **Garlic** | 2 | **medium cloves, chopped** |
| **Dried red chili flakes** | ¼ | **teaspoon** |
| **Salt** | | **A scant pinch** |
| **Dried pasta** | 1½ | **pounds** |

*Recommended pasta:* **spinach linguine or fettuccine**

Several hours before dinnertime, puree all ingredients except the pasta in a food processor or blender to a thick, homogenous consistency. Store covered in the refrigerator. When ready to eat, put several quarts of water on to boil and bring the pesto to room temperature. Cook the pasta until al dente. Toss the pesto with hot pasta in a warm bowl until well distributed. Garnish with finely chopped fresh basil or parsley, if desired.

---

### Each serving provides:

| 402 | Calories | 65 g | Carbohydrate |
|---|---|---|---|
| 13 g | Protein | 118 mg | Sodium |
| 9 g | Fat | 5 mg | Cholesterol |

---

# Spinach and Cheese Pesto with Pimiento

*The red and green of this dish make it fun to serve around the holiday season; however, you will enjoy it any time of the year.*

*Yield:* 4 main-course servings

| | | |
|---|---|---|
| **Fresh spinach** | 2 | **pounds (or 1 10-ounce package frozen)** |
| **Plain lowfat yogurt** | ½ | **cup** |
| **Lowfat cottage cheese** | ⅔ | **cup** |
| **Freshly grated nutmeg** | ½ | **teaspoon** |
| **Garlic** | 2 | **medium cloves, minced** |
| **Olive oil** | 4 | **tablespoons** |
| **Pimiento, chopped** | 1 | **4-ounce jar, drained** |
| **Romano cheese, finely grated** | ⅓ | **cup** |
| **Dried pasta** | 12 | **ounces** |

*Recommended pasta:* **linguine or sphaghetti**

Put several quarts of water on to boil for the pasta. If using fresh spinach, carefully wash it, discard the stems, and place the leaves in a steamer rack over a couple of inches of boiling water in a lidded pot. Steam spinach until it wilts. Cool the cooked spinach in a colander, then squeeze out the excess water. (Alternately, thaw the frozen variety and squeeze out the excess water.) The spinach, whether fresh or frozen, must be as dry as possible. Using a food processor, blend the yogurt, cottage cheese, and nutmeg until smooth. Add the spinach, garlic, and 2 tablespoons of the oil and process until just incorporated. Use a double boiler to heat this mixture or place in a pan and cook gently over very low heat, stirring frequently, until heated through. Stir in the pimiento. Meanwhile, cook the pasta until al dente. Drain well and toss with remaining 2 tablespoons oil in a warm bowl. Toss with the pesto until well distributed and serve immediately. Pass Romano at the table and the pepper grinder, if you wish.

---

Each serving provides:

| 553 | Calories | 75 g | Carbohydrate |
| 24 g | Protein | 395 mg | Sodium |
| 18 g | Fat | 10 mg | Cholesterol |

---

# Shiitake and Spinach Pesto with Ginger

*This dish never fails to surprise and delight our friends. The subtle flavor of spinach is enlivened by robust mushrooms, tangy ginger, and rich roasted sesame oil. A delicious journey to the East.*

*Yield:* 8 main-course servings

| | | |
|---|---|---|
| Dried shiitake mushrooms | 1 | ounce |
| Fresh spinach | 1 | bunch (about ¾ pound) |
| Water chestnuts, chopped | ⅓ | cup |
| Fresh ginger, grated | 2 | tablespoons |
| Roasted sesame oil | 2 | tablespoons |
| Soy sauce | 2 | teaspoons |
| Garlic | 2 | medium cloves, chopped |
| Eggs | 3 | large, hard-boiled, finely chopped |
| Sesame seeds | 2 | tablespoons |
| Green onions | 4 | minced |
| Lemon wedges | 1 | per serving |
| Dried pasta | 1½ | pounds |

*Recommended pasta:* **Asian noodle of your choice (for example, soba or lo mein)**

Soak mushrooms in 2 cups hot water an hour or two. Lift them out, reserving soaking water, and wash carefully under a thin stream of running water to remove all grit. Squeeze liquid out of mushrooms and remove the tough stems. Strain mushroom soaking liquid through a paper coffee filter and set aside. Meanwhile, carefully wash the spinach, discard the stems, and place the leaves in a steamer rack over a couple of inches of boiling water in a lidded pot. Steam until it wilts. This may need to be done in several batches, depending on the size of your steamer. When cool, use your hands to squeeze out all liquid. Chop the spinach coarsely. Combine softened mushrooms, cooked spinach, ½ cup mushroom soaking liquid, the water chestnuts, ginger, sesame oil, soy sauce, and garlic in a food processor and puree until thick and smooth. This can be done several hours in advance. Set the pesto aside in the refrigerator, where the flavors will blend.

When ready to eat, bring several quarts of water to a boil and bring the pesto to room temperature. Toast the sesame seeds (see page 20). Cook the pasta until al dente. Drain well. Toss hot noodles with pesto in a warm bowl and sprinkle generously with eggs, sesame seeds, and green onions. Serve at once with lemon wedges.

---

### Each serving provides:

| | | | |
|---|---|---|---|
| 420 | Calories | 72 g | Carbohydrate |
| 16 g | Protein | 152 mg | Sodium |
| 8 g | Fat | 80 mg | Cholesterol |

---

# Dried-Tomato Pesto with Mint

*The almost smoky richness of dried tomatoes combines well with the bright flavors of fresh mint and feta cheese.*

*Yield:* 10 main-course servings

| | |
|---|---|
| Oil-packed dried tomatoes | ¾ cup, loosely packed |
| Fresh mint leaves | ½ cup, firmly packed |
| Raw walnuts, chopped | ½ cup |
| Tomato paste | ⅓ cup |
| Olive oil | ¼ cup |
| Garlic | 2 medium cloves, chopped |
| Salt | A scant pinch |
| Pepper | Several grinds |
| Feta cheese | ½ pound |
| Lemon wedges | 1 per serving |
| Dried pasta | 2 pounds |

*Recommended pasta:* **sturdy tubes or spirals**

Drain as much oil as possible from tomatoes before measuring. Well ahead of serving time (up to several days), puree the tomatoes, mint, walnuts, tomato paste, olive oil, garlic, salt, and pepper. Do not expect a smooth consistency. Store covered in the refrigerator. When ready to eat, put several quarts of water on to boil and bring the pesto to room temperature. Cook the pasta until al dente. Drain well. Toss in a warm bowl with the pesto and the crumbled feta cheese. Serve with lemon wedges and pass the pepper grinder.

---

Each serving provides:

| | | | |
|---|---|---|---|
| 540 | Calories | 79 g | Carbohydrate |
| 17 g | Protein | 348 mg | Sodium |
| 18 g | Fat | 20 mg | Cholesterol |

---

# Soups with Pasta

Soup is an age-old comfort food. By its very nature it is among the most wholesome of cooked fare—well-saturated ingredients are easy to digest, and the broth collects all the nutrients that can be lost during other types of cooking.

Whether simple and refreshing or complex and hearty, pasta soups are particularly satisfying. Except perhaps at their lightest, they can stand alone as a meal in a bowl—with bread and a tart, leafy salad rounding things out.

The savor of some soups depends on good stock. When you practice the art of making fresh stock, you participate in a timeless international tradition. Many dedicated cooks collect and refrigerate clean vegetable parings for a few days—including the skins of well-scrubbed potatoes. These are combined in fresh water and simmered gently an hour or so to yield, when strained, a tasty and delicate broth which is a fine soup base. When you steam vegetables, save the steaming water to add to your stock.

Wherever the recipes in this chapter call for water, this type of homemade stock can be used with delicious results. Of course, different combinations of vegetables will create distinctly different stocks. Experiment and discover your favorite intermingling of flavors for various soups.

If you haven't the time or inclination to make your own vegetable stock, convenient broth enhancers are available. Many of the recipes in this section use the following preparations:

- *Miso* is a nutritious savory soybean paste that is added to hot soup just before serving (about 1 tablespoon miso to 1 quart soup). Whisk it with a few tablespoons of water, then stir thoroughly into the pot. The miso is suspended in the soup in a lovely light cloud.

- *Vegetable broth cubes* produce a light and savory broth. In some of our recipes, we use a "no salt added" vegetable broth cube. One 0.35-ounce (10 gram) cube contains only 213 mg sodium and makes three 6-ounce servings of broth. The brand we use is imported from Switzerland and is available at health food stores, some large supermarket chains, and imported food outlets. If you can't locate a low-sodium vegetable broth variety, use the regular variety with equally delicious results, though the sodium content will be considerably higher.

Some of our recipes do not call for broth enhancers. The soup ingredients will break up a bit as they cook, blending and incorporating in the simmering water to form a flavorful broth without need of enrichment.

We often prepare soups that include beans as well as pasta. The combination of grains and legumes provides a protein-rich meal, and the flavors and textures of these simple foods are quite compatible. We recommend cooking beans in large quantities and freezing whatever isn't used immediately. Next time cooked beans are needed, they will be readily available without resorting to store-bought. (Basic instructions for cooking dried beans appear on page 9.)

We greatly enjoy the texture and flavor of pastina and use it in many of our soups. These various tiny pasta shapes—which can be as small as a grain of rice—are available at well-stocked supermarkets or Italian food stores. They cook very quickly and distribute well among other ingredients to create a soup with a uniform consistency.

If you have leftover cooked noodles, soup is a fine way to use them. Since they are already tender, add them to the pot only a minute or two before serving, just long enough to heat through.

There is a commonly held notion that soup preparation is time-consuming and difficult, requiring prodigious patience and talent. Nothing could be further from the truth. Begin with fresh water or stock and an abundance of vegetables, add noodles and your favorite seasonings, and discover how simple and satisfying the process can be.

# Basic Vegetable Noodle Soup

*Serve this simple but hearty soup with a crusty whole-grain bread for the perfect winter meal. Don't be alarmed by the amount of garlic indicated in the recipe. It mellows quite magically as it cooks. This soup improves with age for a few days in the refrigerator, or it may be frozen for future use.*

*Yield:* 8 main-course servings

| | | |
|---|---|---|
| Olive oil | 3 | tablespoons |
| Onion | 1 | large, diced |
| Green bell pepper | 1 | large, diced |
| Green cabbage | 1 | cup, finely diced |
| Garlic | 6 | medium cloves, minced |
| Whole tomatoes | 1 | 28-ounce can |
| Water | 8 | cups |
| Low-sodium vegetable broth cubes | 2 | |
| Dried basil | 2 | tablespoons |
| Dried oregano | 1 | tablespoon |
| Dried thyme | ½ | teaspoon |
| Soy sauce | 3 | tablespoons |
| Bay leaves | 2 | |
| Salt | ½ | teaspoon |
| Pepper | | A few grinds |
| Carrots | 2 | medium, diced |
| Mushrooms | ½ | pound, sliced |
| Broccoli, chopped | 3 | cups, loosely packed |
| Dried pastina | ¼ | cup |
| Parmesan cheese, finely grated | 1 | cup |
| Dried pasta | 8 | ounces |

***Recommended pasta:*** **egg noodles or any ribbon variety**

Heat the olive oil in a stockpot and sauté the onion, bell pepper, cabbage, and garlic about 5 minutes. Add the tomatoes with their juice and the water, along with the broth cubes, basil, oregano, thyme, soy sauce, bay leaves, salt, and a few grinds of pepper. Bring to a boil over medium heat. Reduce heat and simmer, uncovered, 20 minutes. Add the carrots, mushrooms, and 8 ounces of pasta (not pastina) to the soup and simmer 5 minutes. Add the broccoli and pastina and simmer just until noodles and pastina are tender. Serve with a generous sprinkling of grated Parmesan.

| Each serving provides: | | | |
|---|---|---|---|
| 255 | Calories | 39 g | Carbohydrate |
| 9 g | Protein | 763 mg | Sodium |
| 8 g | Fat | 27 mg | Cholesterol |

# ✔ Green Pastina Soup

*Simple, nutritious, and delicious, pastina in vegetable and egg broth is at once traditional and thoroughly modern. This makes a light starter course for a dinner party, or a satisfying luncheon main course for 4.*

*Yield:* 6 first-course servings

| | |
|---|---|
| **Fresh chard** | 1 bunch (about ¾ pound) |
| **Butter** | 2 tablespoons |
| **Garlic** | 3 medium cloves, minced |
| **Zucchini** | 1 medium, finely diced |
| **Water** | 6 cups |
| **Soy sauce** | 3 tablespoons |
| **Low-sodium vegetable broth cube** | 1 |
| **Cayenne pepper** | ⅛ teaspoon |
| **Dried pastina** | ½ cup |
| **Egg** | 1, lightly beaten |
| **Parmesan cheese, finely grated** | ½ cup |

Carefully wash the chard leaves, spin dry, and chop to yield about 2 cups. Melt the butter in a stockpot and sauté the garlic briefly, then add the chard and zucchini. Stir and sauté 3–4 minutes, until the vegetables begin to release their juices, then add the water, soy sauce, broth cube, and cayenne. Bring to a simmer over medium-high heat. When bubbling, add the pastina and cook until tender. Turn off the heat and stir the egg into the pot in a slow, thin stream. It will cook as it hits the hot broth and form strands among the pastina and vegetables.* Serve immediately, passing Parmesan to sprinkle on top.

| | Each serving provides: | | |
|---|---|---|---|
| 151 | Calories | 15 g | Carbohydrate |
| 7 g | Protein | 621 mg | Sodium |
| 7 g | Fat | 53 mg | Cholesterol |

*Due to the controversy concerning raw eggs and salmonella bacteria, add eggs when the sauce is very hot, *not* warm. For further information, contact your local office of the U.S. Department of Agriculture.

# Cream of Spinach Soup with Stars

*Early spring is the perfect time to make this soup. The flavor and texture are light, delicate, and fresh—just like the season. Use young spinach and freshly grated nutmeg, if possible, to achieve the optimum flavor.*

*Yield:* 6 first-course servings

| | | |
|---|---|---|
| Fresh spinach | ½ | pound |
| Butter | 3 | tablespoons |
| Onion | 1 | medium, finely chopped |
| Garlic | 2 | medium cloves, minced |
| Ground cumin | 1 | teaspoon |
| Dry sherry | 1 | tablespoon |
| Water | 4 | cups |
| Low-sodium vegetable broth cube | 1 | |
| Salt | ¼ | teaspoon |
| Pepper | | A few grinds |
| Dried star pastina | ⅓ | cup |
| Lowfat milk | 2 | cups |
| Freshly grated nutmeg | | A pinch |
| Lemon peel, finely grated | ½ | teaspoon |
| Lemon wedges | 1 | per serving |

Carefully wash the spinach and discard stems. Melt the butter in a stockpot and add the onion, garlic, cumin, and sherry. Sauté about 2 minutes. Add the water, vegetable broth cube, spinach leaves, salt, and pepper. Bring to a boil, cover, and cook 5 minutes. Puree in a blender or food processor; this may need to be done in several batches. Return the soup to the pot and bring back to a boil. Add the pastina, reduce heat, and simmer, uncovered, 5 more minutes. Stir often while the pastina cooks so it does not sink to the bottom. Add the milk, nutmeg, and lemon peel. Heat through and serve with lemon wedges.

Each serving provides:

| 155 | Calories | 15 g | Carbohydrate |
|-----|----------|------|--------------|
| 6 g | Protein | 284 mg | Sodium |
| 8 g | Fat | 19 mg | Cholesterol |

# ✔ Pastina and Pea Soup

*The preparation time for this soup is so short you can hardly believe it is homemade, from scratch! Serve as a starter course or with French bread and cheese as a quick and delightful lunch or light supper.*

*Yield:* 6 first-course servings

| | | |
|---|---|---|
| Olive oil | 2 | tablespoons |
| Garlic | 3 | medium cloves, minced |
| Onion | 1 | medium, finely diced |
| Water | 6 | cups |
| Low-sodium vegetable broth cubes | 2 | |
| Dried tarragon | 1 | teaspoon |
| White wine | ½ | cup |
| Dried pastina | 1 | cup |
| Half-and-half | ½ | cup |
| Peas, fresh or frozen | 1 | cup |
| Parmesan cheese, finely grated | ½ | cup |

In a large stockpot, sauté the garlic and onion in the olive oil several minutes. Add the water and vegetable broth cubes and bring to a boil over medium-high heat. Stir in the tarragon and wine, reduce heat, and simmer 5 minutes. Bring back to a boil and add the pastina. Cook 4–5 minutes, until al dente. Stir in the half-and-half, peas, and Parmesan. Heat through and serve.

Each serving provides:

| | | | |
|---|---|---|---|
| 264 | Calories | 28 g | Carbohydrate |
| 10 g | Protein | 235 mg | Sodium |
| 11 g | Fat | 14 mg | Cholesterol |

# Creamy Cauliflower Rosemary Soup with Pastina

*This soup was concocted at a moment's notice using the simple ingredients that happened to be on hand. It has become a winter favorite.*

*Yield:* 8 first-course servings

| | | |
|---|---|---|
| Cauliflower | 1 | small |
| Green onions | 7 | |
| Butter | 2 | tablespoons |
| Dried rosemary | 1½ | teaspoons |
| Garlic | 2 | medium cloves, minced |
| Mushrooms | ½ | pound, thickly sliced |
| Salt | ½ | teaspoon |
| Flour | 1 | tablespoon |
| Water | 2½ | cups |
| Lowfat milk | 2½ | cups |
| Brandy | ¼ | cup |
| Soy sauce | 2 | tablespoons |
| Cayenne pepper | ¼ | teaspoon |
| Dried pastina | ½ | cup |
| Parmesan cheese, finely grated | 1 | cup |

Cut the cauliflower into bite-size florets and finely dice the stem portion. Remove all but about 2 inches of the green portion of onions, and cut the remainder into 1-inch lengths. Melt the butter in a heavy stockpot over low heat. Add the rosemary and garlic. Stir and sauté 1 minute before adding cauliflower, green onions, and mushrooms. Sprinkle the salt over the vegetables and sauté, stirring occasionally, about 7 minutes. Sprinkle the flour over the contents of the pan and stir to distribute. Add the water, milk, brandy, soy sauce, and cayenne. Cover and bring to a simmer over medium heat. When bubbling, add the pastina and simmer, uncovered, 5 minutes or so, until it is tender. Serve at once with Parmesan to sprinkle on top.

---

Each serving provides:

| 192 | Calories | 16 g | Carbohydrate |
|---|---|---|---|
| 10 g | Protein | 694 mg | Sodium |
| 8 g | Fat | 20 mg | Cholesterol |

---

# ✔ Carrot Curry Soup with Couscous

*This soup is delicate but full-flavored. Be sure to dice the vegetables very finely to achieve the consistency needed to blend the flavors and please the eye.*

*Yield:* 6 main-course servings

| Butter | 2 | tablespoons |
|---|---|---|
| Onion | 1 | small, finely diced |
| Carrots | 3 | medium, finely diced |
| Red bell pepper | 1 | medium, finely diced |
| Curry powder | 4 | teaspoons |
| Water | 6 | cups |
| Low-sodium vegetable broth cubes | 2 | |
| Dried couscous | ½ | cup |
| Plain lowfat yogurt | 1 | cup |
| Lowfat milk | 1 | cup |
| Fresh cilantro, minced | 2 | tablespoons |

Melt the butter in a large stockpot. Add the vegetables and sauté over very low heat 3–4 minutes. Stir in the curry powder and cook for a moment or two. Add the water and vegetable broth cubes and bring to a boil. Reduce heat, cover, and simmer 10 minutes. Add the couscous, stir, and cover. Continue to

*The Best 125 Meatless Pasta Dishes*

cook 6 minutes. Meanwhile, whisk together the yogurt and milk in a bowl. Add a few tablespoons of the hot soup to the yogurt mixture and stir in. Add a little more hot soup, and stir again. The idea is to gradually heat the yogurt so it does not curdle when added to the soup. When a warm, thin consistency is achieved, stir the yogurt mixture into the soup. Heat through. Stir in the cilantro and serve.

---

Each serving provides:

| | | | |
|---|---|---|---|
| 178 | Calories | 23 g | Carbohydrate |
| 7 g | Protein | 172 mg | Sodium |
| 6 g | Fat | 14 mg | Cholesterol |

---

# Spicy Zucchini Noodle Soup with Avocado Salsa

*You will enjoy the interplay of textures created when this hot soup is topped with the fresh salsa.*

*Yield:* 6 main-course servings

### The salsa

| | | |
|---|---|---|
| Cumin seeds | 1 | teaspoon |
| Avocado, firmly ripe | 1 | medium, peeled and diced |
| Lemon juice | 2 | tablespoons |
| Fresh tomatoes | 2 | medium, diced |
| Green onions | 3 | |
| Garlic | 1 | medium clove, minced |
| Salt | ¼ | teaspoon |
| Cayenne pepper | ⅛ | teaspoon |

*The soup*

| | | |
|---|---|---|
| Olive oil | 2 | tablespoons |
| Garlic | 3 | medium cloves, minced |
| Chili powder | ½ | teaspoon |
| Ground cumin | 1 | teaspoon |
| Onion | 1 | large, coarsely chopped |
| Zucchini | 2 | medium, diced |
| Red bell pepper | 1 | small, diced |
| Dried tomatoes, slivered | ¼ | cup, loosely packed |
| Fresh cilantro, minced | ¼ | cup |
| Water | 3 | cups |
| Salt | ½ | teaspoon |
| Buttermilk or plain lowfat yogurt | 1 | cup |
| Parmesan cheese, finely grated | ½ | cup |
| Dried pasta | 12 | ounces |

*Recommended pasta:* whole wheat ribbons, spirals, or shells

An hour or two before serving time, make the salsa. You must use perfectly ripe tomatoes and avocado. The tomatoes should be a uniform bright red and the avocado should yield easily but only slightly to pressure when squeezed. Toast the cumin seeds (see page 20) and set aside. Toss the avocado with the lemon juice. Add the tomatoes with their juice, to the avocado. Slice the white portion of the onions and a couple of inches of the green into very thin rounds. Add to the salsa, along with the cumin seeds, garlic, salt, and cayenne. Stir gently to combine well, then cover and set aside at room temperature so the flavors can blend.

Half an hour before serving time, put pasta water on to boil in a pot other than the one you will use for the soup. Heat the olive oil in a stockpot, add the garlic, chili powder, and ground cumin, and stir for a moment or two before adding the onion, zucchini, bell pepper, dried tomatoes, and cilantro. Sauté over medium high heat 5 minutes, stirring frequently. Add the water and the salt, bring to a boil, reduce heat, and simmer, uncovered, 10 minutes. Meanwhile, boil the noodles in the pasta water until al dente. Drain well and keep warm until needed. When the soup cooking time is up, whisk a few tablespoons of the hot broth into a bowl with the buttermilk or yogurt, then add the mixture slowly to the soup. Immediately turn off the heat, add half the Parmesan, and stir. Divide the noodles between 6 large bowls. Ladle the soup over the noodles, scoop a good amount of the salsa on top, and sprinkle with a little Parmesan.

---

Each serving provides:

| 392 | Calories | 57 g | Carbohydrate |
|---|---|---|---|
| 16 g | Protein | 490 mg | Sodium |
| 14 g | Fat | 8 mg | Cholesterol |

---

# ✔ Pesto Tortellini Soup

*This soup has a sensual feel to it; a great meal for a quiet, romantic evening. Serve with a butter leaf salad and a chardonnay.*

*Yield:* 2 main-course servings

| | |
|---|---|
| **Fresh spinach and cheese tortellini** | 3 ounces |
| **Water** | 1½ cups |
| **Low-sodium vegetable broth cube** | ½ cube |
| **Lowfat milk (2%)** | ½ cup |
| **Basil Pesto** | ¼ cup (see page 32) |
| **Fresh basil leaves (optional; for garnish)** | Several leaves |

Bring a quart of water to a boil and cook the tortellini until al dente. Drain and set aside. Combine the water, the vegetable broth cube, milk, and pesto in a medium-size pan and bring to a simmer over medium heat. Add the cooked tortellini and simmer a moment longer. Remove from the heat, garnish with the fresh basil, and serve.

---

### Each serving provides:

| | | | |
|---|---|---|---|
| 342 | Calories | 31 g | Carbohydrate |
| 16 g | Protein | 454 mg | Sodium |
| 19 g | Fat | 35 mg | Cholesterol |

---

# Soba in Broth with Fried Vegetables and *Age*

*This dish calls for the puffy deep-fried tofu called* age. *Asian markets carry it fresh, often in bulk. Do not substitute the canned variety. If you are unable to find fresh* age, *use cubed firm tofu in its place. You can substitute vermicelli if you can't locate buckwheat soba.*

*Yield:* 4 main-course servings

### The soba topping

| | | |
|---|---|---|
| Roasted sesame oil | 1 | tablespoon |
| Olive oil | 2 | tablespoons |
| Garlic | 4 | medium cloves, minced |
| Dried red chili flakes | ½ | teaspoon |
| Green onions | 3 | |
| Carrot | 1 | large, thinly sliced |
| Broccoli, chopped | 3 | cups, loosely packed |
| Green cabbage, diced | 2 | cups |
| *Age*, diced | 2 | cups |
| Salt | ¼ | teaspoon |
| Fresh cilantro, minced | ¼ | cup |
| Soba or vermicelli | 8 | ounces |

### The broth

| | | |
|---|---|---|
| Sesame seeds | 2 | tablespoons |
| Water | 3 | cups, plus ¼ cup |
| Mirin or sweet sherry | ¼ | cup |
| Low-sodium vegetable broth cube | 1 | |
| Soy sauce | 1 | tablespoon |
| Miso | 1 | tablespoon |

Put several quarts of water on to boil for the soba. Use the white portion of the onions and about 2 inches of the green, cut into 1-inch lengths. Heat the oils in a high-walled skillet. Sauté the garlic and chili flakes a few moments, then add the onions and carrot. Stir and sauté over medium heat 5 minutes. Add the broccoli, cabbage, *age,* and salt. Stir and sauté 10 minutes longer (you want the vegetables to brown a bit). Turn off the heat, stir in the cilantro, and set aside. Meanwhile, put the soba in the boiling water and cook until soft; buckwheat flour can have a gritty texture when not completely cooked.

While the noodles cook, make the broth. Toast the sesame seeds (see page 20). In a medium-size saucepan combine 3 cups water with the mirin, broth cube, toasted sesame seeds, and soy sauce. Heat to a simmer. Meanwhile, whisk the miso with ¼ cup water until a smooth paste consistency is achieved. When the broth is simmering, turn off the heat and stir in the miso paste. A beautiful cloudy effect will result. Warm 4 deep bowls. Divide the cooked and drained soba among the bowls. Ladle broth into the bowls to just cover the noodles. Top with fried vegetables and serve. You can pass additional soy sauce at the table, if you wish.

| Each serving provides: | | | |
|---|---|---|---|
| 888 | Calories* | 67 g | Carbohydrate |
| 37 g | Protein | 719 mg | Sodium |
| 55 g | Fat | 0 mg | Cholesterol |

*Because this is high in calories, you might want to save this for a special occasion.

# French Onion Soup with Pasta

*This soup could also be served as a hearty main course for 4. For us, it has replaced the traditional chicken noodle soup as the cure for the common cold, but you do not need to be sick to enjoy it.*

*Yield:* 8 first-course servings

| | | |
|---|---|---|
| **Canola oil** | ¼ | **cup** |
| **Onions** | 5 | **medium, coarsely chopped** |
| **Bay leaves** | 2 | **whole** |
| **Water** | 2 | **cups, plus 8 cups** |
| **Soy sauce** | 2 | **tablespoons** |
| **Worcestershire sauce** | 1 | **tablespoon** |
| **Pickapeppa sauce (optional)** | 1 | **teaspoon** |
| **Low-sodium vegetable broth cubes** | 3 | |
| **Lemon peel, finely grated** | ½ | **teaspoon** |
| **Jarlsberg cheese, grated (optional)** | 1½ | **cups** |
| **Dried pasta** | 1 | **cup** |

*Recommended pasta:* any small soup pasta such as small shells or tripolini

Heat the oil in a large stockpot over medium heat. Add the onions and bay leaves; reduce heat and cook gently, stirring often, about 10 minutes, until the onions are translucent and golden (do not brown them). Meanwhile, in a small saucepan, bring 2 cups water to a boil; add the soy sauce, Worcestershire,

Pickapeppa, and broth cubes. When the onions are golden, remove the bay leaves and add the lemon peel. Pour in the broth
mixture and 8 additional cups water. Bring to a boil, then reduce heat. Simmer, covered, over low heat 1¼ hours. Remove
the lid, increase the heat to a boil, add the pasta, and cook until
al dente. Ladle the soup into individual ovenproof serving
bowls. Top with the cheese and place under the broiler for a
minute or so to melt it. Serve immediately. (This soup is also
delightful without the cheese.)

---

Each serving provides:

| | | | |
|---|---|---|---|
| 180 | Calories | 21 g | Carbohydrate |
| 5 g | Protein | 367 mg | Sodium |
| 8 g | Fat | 0 mg | Cholesterol |

---

# Savory Pumpkin and Pasta Soup

*Pumpkin is high in beta carotene and fiber, which makes it especially nutritious. This recipe calls for canned pumpkin because it is available all year, but you can use cooked and pureed fresh pumpkin. The soup's flavor is wonderful, its texture light and creamy. We suggest either of two different garnishes. The toasted walnuts lend a woodsy accent that complements the nutmeg and allspice. Try the cilantro and lemon for a lighter, summer version. Serve with a merlot and hot rolls.*

*Yield:* 6 main-course servings

| | | |
|---|---|---|
| Pumpkin | 1 | 29-ounce can or 4 cups fresh puree |
| Garlic | 2 | medium cloves, minced |
| Water | 3½ | cups |
| Low-sodium vegetable broth cube | 1 | |
| Lowfat milk | 2 | cups |
| Dried pastina | ¼ | cup |
| Ground nutmeg | | Scant ⅛ teaspoon |
| Ground allspice | | Scant ⅛ teaspoon |
| Salt and pepper | | To taste |
| Fresh parsley, finely minced | ¾ | cup |
| Romano cheese, finely grated | 1 | cup |
| Butter | 3 | tablespoons |
| Plain lowfat yogurt | 1 | cup |

| | | |
|---|---|---|
| Raw walnuts, minced | ¼ | cup |
| or | | |
| Fresh cilantro, minced | ⅓ | cup |
| Lemon wedges | 1 | per serving |

In a large stockpot, combine the pumpkin, garlic, water, vegetable broth cube, and milk. Bring to a boil and stir in the pastina. Cook until al dente, about 7 minutes, then add the nutmeg, allspice, salt, pepper, and parsley. Remove the pan from the heat and stir in the Romano and butter. Whisk a few tablespoons of hot soup into the yogurt. Whisk in a few more tablespoons of hot soup. The idea is to gradually heat the yogurt so it does not curdle when added to the soup. When a warm, thin consistency is achieved, stir the yogurt mixture into the soup. Serve immediately in heated bowls with the garnish of your choice. If you plan to offer the walnut garnish, toast the chopped walnuts ahead of time (see page 20).

---

Each serving provides:

| | | | |
|---|---|---|---|
| 257 | Calories | 27 g | Carbohydrate |
| 12 g | Protein | 333 mg | Sodium |
| 12 g | Fat | 35 mg | Cholesterol |

---

# Caldo Verde with Pasta and Port

*A traditional Portuguese soup is transformed from humble to haute with the addition of port wine and pasta. Yes, it is a lot of garlic, but it mellows completely as it cooks and softens. As the name implies, the finished soup is a lovely spring green, so use a white noodle for color contrast. This soup is quite hearty, perfect for a cold evening when you want a meal that sticks to the ribs.*

*Yield:* 8 main-course servings

| | | |
|---|---|---|
| **Fresh kale** | ½ | **pound** |
| **Garlic** | 1 | **bulb (12 medium cloves)** |
| **Russet potatoes** | 2 | **pounds, peeled and diced** |
| **Onion** | 1 | **large, coarsely chopped** |
| **Water** | 6 | **cups** |
| **Salt** | 1 | **teaspoon** |
| **Pepper** | | **A few grinds** |
| **Olive oil** | 3 | **tablespoons** |
| **Port** | ¾ | **cup** |
| **Parmesan cheese, finely grated** | 3 | **tablespoons** |
| **Lemon wedges** | 1 | **per serving** |
| **Dried pasta** | 8 | **ounces** |

*Recommended pasta:* egg noodles are ideal, or any ribbon broken into short lengths

Wash the kale, discard the toughest part of the stems, and tear leaves into large pieces. Break the garlic bulb into individual cloves and peel them. In a stockpot, combine the potatoes, onion, kale, whole garlic cloves, and water. Stir in the salt and a few grinds of pepper and bring to a boil over medium-high

*The Best 125 Meatless Pasta Dishes*

heat. Reduce heat to low and simmer, covered, an hour or so, until all the vegetables are quite soft. Meanwhile, bring a few quarts of water to a boil in a separate pot and cook the pasta until al dente. Be careful not to overcook, as the slightly chewy texture of the noodles is important to the success of this dish. Drain well, toss with 1 tablespoon of the olive oil, and set aside. Puree the soup in a blender or food processor and return to the pot—this will have to be done in two batches. Whisk port, 2 tablespoons olive oil, and Parmesan into the pureed soup. Taste and add more salt and pepper, if desired. Stir in the cooked noodles and heat through. Serve very hot with lemon wedges and additional Parmesan, if desired.

---

Each serving provides:

| 306 | Calories | 48 g | Carbohydrate |
|---|---|---|---|
| 8 g | Protein | 342 mg | Sodium |
| 7 g | Fat | 29 mg | Cholesterol |

---

# Red Lentil and Pasta Soup

*Red lentils are not as common as the brown variety, but they are worth looking for. Many gourmet food stores carry them, as well as natural food stores. The flavor is lighter and more delicate, and the cooking time shorter. This recipe calls for finely chopped onions, and this is very important to the outcome of the soup. Use a food processor if you have one. This soup could also be served as a light but nourishing main course.*

*Yield:* 6 first-course servings

| | | |
|---|---|---|
| Red lentils | ½ | cup |
| Butter | 3 | tablespoons |
| Onion | 1 | large, finely chopped |
| Dried chervil | 1 | teaspoon |
| Dried tarragon | 1 | teaspoon |
| Low-sodium vegetable broth cubes | 2 | |
| Hot water | 7 | cups |
| Port | ½ | cup |
| Dried pastina | ½ | cup |

Sort and rinse the lentils and soak them, covered, in 1 cup boiling water 30 minutes. Meanwhile, melt the butter in a large stockpot over low heat and sauté the onion about 4 minutes, until golden. Add the chervil and tarragon; stir to distribute. Dissolve the broth cubes in 2 cups hot water and pour it into the soup pot. Add the remaining 5 cups hot water and bring to a boil. Pour in the lentils, along with their soaking liquid, and return to a boil. Reduce heat. Simmer, uncovered, until lentils are soft, about 25 minutes. Bring the pot back to a strong boil and stir in the pastina. Continue to cook about 4 minutes, until the pastina is al dente. Stir in the port and serve in heated bowls.

| Each serving provides: | | | |
|---|---|---|---|
| 227 | Calories | 27 g | Carbohydrate |
| 8 g | Protein | 135 mg | Sodium |
| 7 g | Fat | 16 mg | Cholesterol |

# Tomato Cannellini Bean Soup with Noodles

*The body of this soup is thick and chunky. It is sure to satisfy large appetites. Cannellini beans are available in any Italian grocery store. If you are unable to find them, substitute navy beans.*

*Yield:* 6 main-course servings

| | |
|---|---|
| Dried cannellini or navy beans | ½ cup |
| Olive oil | 2 tablespoons |
| Garlic | 2 medium cloves, minced |
| Onion | 1 medium, coarsely chopped |
| Stewed tomatoes | 1 16-ounce can |
| Tomato paste | 1 6-ounce can |
| Water | 7 cups |
| Dried oregano | 2 tablespoons |
| Salt and pepper | To taste |
| Broccoli florets | 2 cups, loosely packed |
| Mushrooms | ½ pound, sliced |
| Parmesan cheese, finely grated | ¾ cup |
| Dried pasta | ½ cup |

*Recommended pasta:* any small soup-style pasta, such as tubes or mini-bowties

Sort and rinse the beans and soak several hours or overnight. Drain. In a large stockpot, gently heat the olive oil. Add the garlic and onion and sauté over low heat several minutes. Add the beans, stewed tomatoes and their liquid, tomato paste, the water, and oregano. Bring to a boil, reduce heat, and simmer 25 minutes, until the beans are tender but not fully cooked, stirring occasionally. Salt and pepper can be added to taste. Add the broccoli and mushrooms to the soup, along with the pasta. Increase the heat to a boil, stir, and turn down to a rapid simmer. Simmer until pasta is al dente. Serve very hot, passing the Parmesan.

---

Each serving provides:

| | | | |
|---|---|---|---|
| 273 | Calories | 36 g | Carbohydrate |
| 15 g | Protein | 660 mg | Sodium |
| 9 g | Fat | 10 mg | Cholesterol |

---

# Spinach, Lima Bean, and Pasta Soup

*The blending of red, white, and green in this soup pleases the eye as much as the flavors please the palate. Make it when you find really fresh and beautiful spinach at the market.*

*Yield:* 8 main-course servings

**The beans**

| | | |
|---|---|---|
| Dried lima beans | 2 | cups |
| Bay leaves | 3 | |
| Garlic | 1 | large clove, crushed |

**The soup**

| | | |
|---|---|---|
| Fresh spinach | 2 | bunches (about 1½ pounds) |
| Olive oil | 3 | tablespoons |
| Red bell pepper | 1 | medium, coarsely chopped |
| Onion | 1 | medium, coarsely chopped |
| Garlic | 2 | medium cloves, minced |
| Dried basil | 1 | tablespoon |
| Salt | ½ | teaspoon |
| Water | 4 | cups |
| Soy sauce | 2 | tablespoons |
| Cayenne pepper | ¼ | teaspoon |
| Parmesan cheese, finely grated | ½ | cup |
| Dried pasta | 8 | ounces |

*Recommended pasta:* shells, bowties, or spirals

Sort and rinse the beans and soak several hours or overnight. Drain off the soaking water and boil the beans in a quart or so of fresh water 45 minutes, along with the bay leaves and crushed garlic clove. Drain, reserving 2 cups of the cooking liquid. Carefully wash the spinach, discard the stems, and coarsely chop. In a stockpot, heat the olive oil and add the bell pepper, onion, garlic, and basil. Stir and sauté about 5 minutes. Stir in the spinach, sprinkle with the salt, cover, and steam about 5 minutes. Add the beans, 4 cups water, the reserved bean cooking liquid, soy sauce, and cayenne. Simmer, uncovered, over medium heat 15 minutes. Meanwhile, bring a few quarts of water to a boil and cook the pasta until al dente. Drain the pasta and stir it into the soup. Serve hot, passing the Parmesan.

Each serving provides:

| 248 | Calories | 34 g | Carbohydrate |
| 11 g | Protein | 562 mg | Sodium |
| 8 g | Fat | 5 mg | Cholesterol |

# Minestrone with Rosemary Pesto

*Soups are such a wonderful blending of diverse ingredients. This one calls on one unexpected guest, namely Rosemary Pesto!*

*Yield:* 8 main-course servings

| | | |
|---|---|---|
| Dried cannellini or navy beans | ½ | cup |
| Olive oil | 3 | tablespoons |
| Celery | 3 | ribs, finely diced |
| Onion | 1 | large, finely diced |
| Green cabbage, shredded | 4 | cups |
| Carrot | 1 | large, finely diced |
| Stewed tomatoes | 1 | 16-ounce can |
| Bay leaves | 3 | |
| Salt and pepper | | To taste |
| Water | 10 | cups |
| Low-sodium vegetable broth cube | 1 | |
| Rosemary Pesto | 4 | tablespoons (see page 33) |
| Dried pasta | ½ | cup |

*Recommended pasta:* any small soup shape, such as shells, bowties, or tripolini

Soak the beans several hours or overnight. Drain. Heat the olive oil in a large stockpot. Sauté the celery and onion a few minutes, until just tender. Add the beans, cabbage, carrot, and stewed tomatoes. Cook over low heat several minutes, stirring often. Add 8 cups water, broth cube, bay leaves, salt, and pepper. Bring to a boil over medium heat. Reduce heat, cover, and simmer 1¼ hours. Stir occasionally. When the beans are tender, add 2 cups boiling water and the pasta. Bring to a rapid simmer and cook until pasta is al dente. Stir in the pesto. Remove from the heat and let stand a few minutes before serving.

---

Each serving provides:

| 203 | Calories | 23 g | Carbohydrate |
|---|---|---|---|
| 6 g | Protein | 227 mg | Sodium |
| 10 g | Fat | 1 mg | Cholesterol |

---

# Two-Bean Zuppa

*Here, the simple ingredients produce a hearty, stewlike soup that is very filling. If you want to make it in a hurry, substitute canned beans for the dried ones. One cup of each bean will do; drain and rinse before using.*

*Yield:* 6 main-course servings

| | | |
|---|---|---|
| Dried garbanzo beans (chickpeas) | ½ | cup |
| Dried kidney beans | ½ | cup |
| Water | 10 | cups |
| Low-sodium vegetable broth cube | 1 | |
| Olive oil | 3 | tablespoons |
| Onions | 2 | medium, finely diced |
| Garlic | 4 | medium cloves, minced |
| Canned stewed tomatoes | 1 | cup |
| Basil Pesto | ½ | cup (see page 32) |
| Lowfat milk | 1 | cup |
| Dried pasta | 1 | cup |

*Recommended pasta:* ziti or other small tube variety

Sort and rinse the beans and soak them several hours or overnight. Drain. Combine beans, 8 cups water, and the vegetable broth cube in a large pot. Bring to a boil. Reduce heat and maintain at a simmer. Heat the olive oil in a skillet and sauté the onions and garlic until the onions are just transparent. Add to the beans and cook about 45 minutes, until the beans are soft but not mushy. Stir in the tomatoes and pesto; simmer, uncovered, 10 minutes. Bring up to a boil; add 2 cups boiling water and the pasta. Cook until the pasta is al dente, stirring occasionally. Just before serving, add the milk and heat through.

---

Each serving provides:

| 410 | Calories | 46 g | Carbohydrate |
|-----|----------|------|--------------|
| 16 g | Protein | 325 mg | Sodium |
| 19 g | Fat | 6 mg | Cholesterol |

---

# Curried Tomato Soup with Pasta and Garbanzos

*This beautiful red soup is hearty and warming—perfect for a rainy day.*

*Yield:* 8 main-course servings

**The beans**

| | | |
|---|---|---|
| Dried garbanzo beans (chickpeas) | 1 | cup |
| Garlic | 3 | medium cloves, crushed |
| Bay leaves | 2 | |
| Dried red chili flakes | 1 | teaspoon |

**The soup**

| | | |
|---|---|---|
| Butter | 3 | tablespoons |
| Garlic | 4 | medium cloves, minced |
| Onion | 1 | medium, coarsely chopped |
| Dried thyme | 1 | teaspoon |
| Curry powder | 2–3 | tablespoons |
| Carrots | 2 | medium, diced |
| Zucchini | 1 | medium, diced |
| Green bell pepper | 1 | medium, finely chopped |

| Broccoli, chopped | 3 | cups, loosely packed |
|---|---|---|
| Whole tomatoes | 1 | 28-ounce can |
| Water | 9 | cups |
| Soy sauce | 2 | tablespoons |
| Salt | ½ | teaspoon |
| Cayenne | | To taste |
| Dry red wine | 1 | cup |
| Plain lowfat yogurt | 1 | cup |
| Dried pasta | 8 | ounces |

*Recommended pasta:* small shells, elbows, or tubes

Sort and rinse the beans and soak several hours or overnight. Drain. Cover beans with fresh water in a large pot. Add the crushed garlic, bay leaves, and chili flakes. Cover and simmer 1 hour, or until beans are tender but not mushy. Drain the beans and set aside.

Melt the butter in a stockpot, add the garlic, onion, thyme, and 2 tablespoons curry powder (the total amount of curry you use will depend on the intensity of the brand you buy). Stir and sauté a minute or two, then add the carrots, zucchini, bell pepper, and broccoli. Stir and sauté about 5 minutes longer. Add the tomatoes, water, soy sauce, and salt. Add a little cayenne pepper or additional curry powder if you want a spicier soup. Bring the soup to a simmer over medium-high heat. Meanwhile, boil a few quarts of water in a separate pot and cook the pasta until al dente. Drain well, toss with a tablespoon of olive oil, and set aside. When soup is simmering, add the wine and cooked garbanzos and cook, uncovered, 5 minutes. Turn off the heat and stir in the cooked pasta. Whisk a few tablespoons of hot soup broth into the yogurt in a small bowl. Add a few more tablespoons of hot soup and whisk again. The idea is to heat the yogurt gradually so it does not curdle when added to the soup. When a warm, thin consistency is achieved, gently stir it into the soup. Serve very hot.

---

Each serving provides:

| 335 | Calories | 51 g | Carbohydrate |
| 13 g | Protein | 646 mg | Sodium |
| 7 g | Fat | 13 mg | Cholesterol |

---

# Pasta Salads

Like its cousin, potato salad, macaroni salad has long been an American picnic standard. Gradually, the classic version— dominated by celery, egg, and mayonnaise—is being replaced by lighter, more inventive concoctions. No longer loyal to old-fashioned elbow and short tube noodles for salad, we draw on a vast array of pasta shapes as inspiration for innovative cold feasts.

Oil is an important component in most pasta salads. We commonly use extra virgin olive oil, which adds a robust olive aroma and flavor. Gourmet oils, such as walnut and sesame, also add distinctive accents that can lend special character to a dish. They are quite powerful, so a little goes a long way.

Specialty vinegars infuse a salad with delicate but unique flavors. They are available in vast variety at well-stocked gourmet food stores, or you can easily make your own. Pack a jar with your choice of herbs and a few peeled and sliced garlic cloves. Cover with heated wine vinegar and cap tightly. Put the jars in a bright spot in your kitchen and let them stand several days, then strain the vinegar through cheesecloth into sterilized decorative jars. Store them in your basement or kitchen cupboard until ready to use. A sprig or two of the fresh herb can be placed in each jar for easy visual identification.

Also deserving mention is rice wine vinegar, available at Asian specialty food stores, which imparts a subtle sweetness. Balsamic vinegar from the Mediterranean region is another distinctive vinegar you may wish to keep on hand for its mellow, woody flavor.

Naturally, a great pasta salad begins with perfectly cooked pasta. Cook it in plenty of boiling water until it is al dente, then cool it by plunging it into a bowl of cold water for a few moments. Drain it well so your flavorful dressing won't be diluted. If you have cooked the noodles before the other salad components are ready, toss them with a little olive oil and set aside—at room temperature if they will be held under an hour, in the refrigerator if longer. Combine the cooled noodles with the other ingredients and toss gently, but thoroughly, to distribute everything evenly. Serve immediately, or allow the salad to marinate a few hours first so the flavors can combine and ripen.

We recommend that pasta salads, particularly those with creamy dressings, be held in the refrigerator if they are not to be eaten immediately. Before serving, allow the refrigerated salad to sit at room temperature an hour or so. The flavors will relax and expand as the salad warms slightly, and the sauce will return to a perfect smooth consistency.

Salads containing raw sliced or chopped mushrooms should marinate no longer than two hours or so, as mushrooms can turn rubbery and darken the mixture to an unappetizing brown. If your salad contains nuts, you may wish to hold them out and add them just before serving to preserve their crunch.

Since macaroni salads are most often served in combination with other foods, at a picnic or a potluck, our suggested serving sizes reflect this. These salads are delicious enough, however, to serve as a main course when you're in the mood for a light and refreshing repast.

So many delicious combinations of flavor, color, and texture are possible. We hope the diversity of salad styles we present here will encourage you to experiment in your own kitchen joyfully and fearlessly.

# Summer-Fresh Pasta Salad

*This salad is lightly dressed with a creamy pesto dressing. The fresh vegetables give it a wonderful light texture and flavor. Make it ahead of time so the flavors can blend, but don't hold it overnight, as the pesto discolors the noodles.*

*Yield:* 8 side-dish servings

**The dressing**

| | |
|---|---|
| Mayonnaise | ¼ cup |
| Light sour cream | ½ cup |
| Basil Pesto | ¼ cup (see page 32) |
| Salt | ½ teaspoon |

**The salad**

| | |
|---|---|
| Olive oil | 1 tablespoon |
| Celery | 2 ribs, diced |
| Red onion, finely diced | ½ cup |
| Black olives, chopped | ⅓ cup |
| Zucchini | 1 medium, diced |
| Fresh parsley, minced | 1 cup |
| Dried pasta | 12 ounces |

*Recommended pasta:* spirals or shells

Whisk together the dressing ingredients and refrigerate to allow flavors to blend while you prepare the rest of the salad. Cook the pasta until al dente. Cool in a bowl of cold water and drain well. Transfer to a large bowl and drizzle with the olive oil. Toss gently to coat the noodles. Add the remaining ingredients and toss well to distribute everything evenly. Pour the dressing over the salad and toss to combine.

Each serving provides:

| 307 | Calories | 38 g | Carbohydrate |
| 9 g | Protein | 284 mg | Sodium |
| 14 g | Fat | 11 mg | Cholesterol |

# Pasta Salad with Broccoli and Mustard Seeds

*This salad combines a considerable quantity of vegetables with the pasta, so it does not come across as too starchy. A great light picnic salad.*

*Yield:* 8 side-dish servings

### The dressing

| | |
|---|---|
| Mustard seeds | 1 tablespoon |
| Olive oil | ½ cup |
| Water | ¼ cup |
| Garlic | 1 medium clove, minced |
| Capers, with juice | 3 tablespoons |
| Lemon juice | 3 tablespoons |
| Salt | ¼ teaspoon |
| Pepper | A few grinds |

### The salad

| | |
|---|---|
| Broccoli florets | 3 cups, loosely packed |
| Broccoli stems, peeled and diced | 1 cup |
| Red bell pepper | 1 medium, finely diced |
| Mushrooms | ½ pound, thinly sliced |
| Parmesan cheese, finely grated | ¼ cup |
| Dried pasta | 8 ounces |

*Recommended pasta:* spirals or tubes

The vegetables should marinate in the dressing a few hours before being combined with the pasta, so begin to prepare the salad well ahead of time. Toast the mustard seeds (see page 20). Whisk together the dressing ingredients until smooth. Set aside. Put a few inches of water in a lidded pot and place a steaming rack over the water. Bring the water to a boil and steam the broccoli florets 3–4 minutes, until barely tender. Cool in a bowl of cold water. Drain well and combine with the raw diced broccoli stems, bell pepper, and dressing in a large bowl. Toss to coat evenly and marinate in the refrigerator. This can be done up to a day in advance. When ready to serve, bring marinated vegetables to room temperature. Cook the pasta until al dente, cool in a bowl of cold water, drain, and toss with the marinated vegetables, the mushrooms, and the cheese.

| Each serving provides: | | | |
|---|---|---|---|
| 270 | Calories | 27 g | Carbohydrate |
| 7 g | Protein | 225 mg | Sodium |
| 16 g | Fat | 2 mg | Cholesterol |

# Pasta Salad with Pesto and Peas

*This is a nice fresh-tasting summer salad, perfect to take along on a picnic.*

*Yield:* 8 side-dish servings

**The dressing**

| | | |
|---|---|---|
| Mayonnaise | 1½ | cups |
| Basil Pesto | ¼ | cup (see page 32) |
| Lemon juice | ¼ | cup |
| Garlic | 2 | medium cloves, minced |

**The salad**

| | | |
|---|---|---|
| Olive oil | 1 | tablespoon |
| Romano cheese, finely grated | 1 | cup |
| Black olives, chopped | ½ | cup, firmly packed |
| Cucumber | 1 | large, peeled, seeded, diced |
| Mushrooms | ½ | pound, sliced |
| Peas, fresh or frozen | 1½ | cups |
| Dried pasta | 12 | ounces |

*Recommended pasta:* **spirals or shells**

This salad will improve if it marinates several hours in the refrigerator, so make it well ahead of time. If using frozen peas, set them out to thaw before beginning. Whisk together the dressing ingredients. Set aside. Bring a large pan of water to a boil and cook the pasta until al dente. Cool in a bowl of cold water and drain well. Transfer to a large bowl and toss with the olive oil. Add the Romano, olives, cucumber, mushrooms, and peas to the pasta and toss well to distribute the ingredients evenly. Pour the dressing over the salad and toss gently but well to coat every noodle.

| Each serving provides: | | | |
|---|---|---|---|
| 595 | Calories | 42 g | Carbohydrate |
| 13 g | Protein | 510 mg | Sodium |
| 43 g | Fat | 37 mg | Cholesterol |

# Mushrooms, Jarlsberg, and Pasta with Tarragon Citrus Dressing

*This delectable raw mushroom feast looks lovely arranged on a platter and garnished with fresh tarragon sprigs and lemon wedges.*

*Yield:* 8 side-dish servings

**The dressing**

| | |
|---|---|
| Olive oil | ⅓ cup |
| Lemon juice | ¼ cup |
| Orange juice | ¼ cup |
| Fresh tarragon leaves, minced | ¼ cup |
| Capers, drained | 3 tablespoons |
| Garlic | 2 medium cloves, minced |
| Prepared mustard | ½ teaspoon |
| Salt | ¼ teaspoon |
| Pepper | A few grinds |

**The salad**

| | |
|---|---|
| Olive oil | 1 tablespoon |
| Mushrooms | ¾ pound, thinly sliced |
| Jarlsberg cheese | 8 ounces, coarsely grated |
| Dried pasta | 8 ounces |

*Recommended pasta:* penne, spirals, or medium shells

Make the dressing first so the flavors can blend. Puree the dressing ingredients in a food processor or blender. Set aside at room temperature. Bring a pot of water to a boil and cook the pasta until al dente. Cool in a bowl of cold water and drain well. Toss with the olive oil in a large bowl. Toss gently with the mushrooms and cheese, then add dressing and toss again.

| Each serving provides: | | | |
|---|---|---|---|
| 315 | Calories | 26 g | Carbohydrate |
| 12 g | Protein | 295 mg | Sodium |
| 18 g | Fat | 18 mg | Cholesterol |

# Tortellini Salad with Roasted Walnuts

*We usually serve macaroni salads as a side dish; however, this stuffed pasta salad makes a satisfying meal in itself. Make it several hours before serving so it can sit at room temperature to allow the flavors to combine. If you wish to make it the night before, refrigerate then let it return to room temperature before serving. The recipe sounds like it has a lot of steps, but it is really very easy to prepare.*

*Yield:* 4 main-course servings

*The dressing*

| | | |
|---|---|---|
| Walnut oil | ⅓ | cup |
| Wine vinegar | 3 | tablespoons |
| Salt and pepper | | To taste |

*The nuts*

| | | |
|---|---|---|
| Olive oil | 2 | tablespoons |
| Garlic | 2 | medium cloves, minced |
| Raw walnuts, chopped | ½ | cup |
| Salt and pepper | | To taste |

*The salad*

| | | |
|---|---|---|
| Fresh parsley, minced | ½ | cup |
| Green bell pepper, finely diced | ¼ | cup |
| Red bell pepper, finely diced | ⅓ | cup |
| Red onion, finely diced | ¼ | cup |
| Celery | 1 | rib, finely diced |
| Parmesan cheese, finely grated | ½ | cup |
| Fresh cheese tortellini | 9 | ounces |

Whisk together the dressing ingredients. Set aside. Heat the olive oil in a small heavy skillet. Add the garlic and cook briefly. Add the walnuts and cook several minutes, stirring frequently. Lightly season with salt and pepper. When walnuts turn golden brown, remove from the heat and drain on paper towels to remove most of the oil. Set aside. Bring several quarts of water with a bit of oil in it to a boil. Cook the tortellini until al dente, drain, and shake gently to remove as much water as possible. In a large bowl, combine the tortellini, parsley, and diced vegetables. Pour the dressing over the salad and toss. Add the walnuts and Parmesan and toss again, gently. (If making this salad well ahead of time, hold out the walnuts and add them just before serving.)

Each serving provides:

| 577 | Calories | 36 g | Carbohydrate |
|---|---|---|---|
| 18 g | Protein | 526 mg | Sodium |
| 41 g | Fat | 45 mg | Cholesterol |

# Cold Pasta in Creamy Garlic Cucumber Sauce

*This salad is for garlic lovers only! Serve small portions as a pungent side dish or as the first course of a strongly seasoned feast.*

*Yield:* 8 side-dish servings

| | | |
|---|---|---|
| Cumin seeds | 1 | tablespoon |
| Plain lowfat yogurt | 1½ | cups |
| Garlic | 4 | medium cloves, minced |
| Red wine vinegar | 1 | tablespoon |
| Salt | ½ | teaspoon |
| Pepper | | A few grinds |
| Cucumbers | 2 | large, peeled and seeded |
| Dried tomatoes, slivered | ¼ | cup, loosely packed |
| Parmesan cheese, finely grated | ½ | cup |
| Dried pasta | 12 | ounces |

*Recommended pasta:* wagon wheels, spirals, or tubes

*The Best 125 Meatless Pasta Dishes*

Make the salad and refrigerate a few hours ahead of serving time, if possible, so the flavors will blend and ripen. Put several quarts of water on to boil for the pasta. Toast the cumin seeds (see page 20). Whisk together the cumin seeds, yogurt, garlic, vinegar, salt, and pepper. Grate the cucumbers into the yogurt mixture and stir in the dried tomatoes and Parmesan. Cook the pasta until al dente, cool in a bowl of cold water, and drain well. In a serving bowl, toss the cooled noodles with the yogurt-cucumber sauce.

Each serving provides:

| | | | |
|---|---|---|---|
| 231 | Calories | 39 g | Carbohydrate |
| 11 g | Protein | 290 mg | Sodium |
| 3 g | Fat | 7 mg | Cholesterol |

# Spicy Eggplant Pasta Salad with Calamata Olives

*We find the balance of sweet, sour, and spicy just right in this distinctive salad. We set out to duplicate a dish we had enjoyed at a gourmet lunch counter in Berkeley. Our own ideas took over and it turned out not the same at all, though just as delicious. This dish is interesting and rich enough to carry a meal as a main course.*

*Yield:* 8 main-course servings

| | | |
|---|---|---|
| Eggplants | 2 | small (about 1½ pounds) |
| Green onions | 7 | |
| Olive oil | 7 | tablespoons |
| Garlic | 4 | medium cloves, minced |
| Dried red chili flakes | 1 | teaspoon |
| Red bell pepper | 1 | medium, thinly sliced |
| Dried oregano | 1 | teaspoon |
| Salt | ¾ | teaspoon |
| Lemon juice | ¼ | cup |
| Balsamic vinegar | 1 | tablespoon |
| Mirin or sweet sherry | 2 | tablespoons |
| Calamata olives, slivered | ½ | cup |
| Fresh parsley, minced | ½ | cup |
| Dried pasta | 1 | pound |

*Recommended pasta:* rigatoni, penne, or other large tubes

Peel the eggplant and cut it into ¼-inch-thick strips about 3 inches in length. Trim all but about 2 inches of the tops from the green onions. Cut in half lengthwise, then into 1-inch pieces. Bring several quarts of water to a boil. Cook the pasta until al dente. Cool in a bowl of cold water, drain well, and toss with 1 tablespoon of the olive oil. Set aside.

Heat 2 tablespoons of the olive oil in a heavy skillet over medium-high heat. Add the garlic and chili flakes and stir to distribute in the oil. Add the eggplant, green onion, and bell pepper; stir. Sprinkle with the oregano and ¼ teaspoon of the salt. Stir and sauté over medium-high heat 15–20 minutes, until vegetables are tender and browning nicely. Transfer to a bowl. Meanwhile, whisk together the remaining 4 tablespoons olive oil, the lemon juice, vinegar, mirin, and remaining ½ teaspoon salt. Pour this dressing over the eggplant mixture in the bowl and let the flavors combine for up to a few hours before tossing with the cooled pasta, the olives, and parsley.

---

### Each serving provides:

| 386 | Calories | 52 g | Carbohydrate |
|------|----------|--------|--------------|
| 9 g | Protein | 513 mg | Sodium |
| 16 g | Fat | 0 mg | Cholesterol |

---

# ✔ Pastina Salad with Romaine and Feta

*Serve this full-flavored salad as a first course, or make a meal of it with French bread and cheese.*

*Yield:* 4 side-dish servings

### The dressing
| | | |
|---|---|---|
| Olive oil | 2 | tablespoons |
| Red wine vinegar | 1 | tablespoon |
| Sugar | 1 | teaspoon |
| Half-and-half | 1 | tablespoon |

### The salad
| | | |
|---|---|---|
| Romaine lettuce, torn | 2 | cups |
| Fresh tomato | 1 | medium, chopped |
| Fresh parsley, minced | ½ | cup |
| Feta cheese, crumbled | ½ | cup |
| Dried pastina | ½ | cup |

Whisk together the olive oil and vinegar until light in color. Add the sugar and half-and-half; whisk to combine. Set aside. Heat a small pan of water and cook the pastina until al dente.

Pay close attention as this will take only a couple of minutes. Cool in a bowl of cold water and drain well. Set aside. Toss the lettuce, tomato, and parsley gently in a bowl. Add the feta and cooked pastina and toss again to combine. Pour the dressing over the salad, toss, and serve.

---

Each serving provides:

| | | | |
|---|---|---|---|
| 201 | Calories | 19 g | Carbohydrate |
| 6 g | Protein | 199 mg | Sodium |
| 11 g | Fat | 16 mg | Cholesterol |

---

# Salad of Olives, Artichokes, Pesto, and Pasta

*This dish really hits the spot when you are in the mood for a creamy, rich, cold salad. Make it several hours before mealtime to allow the flavors to combine. Refrigerate it but return it to room temperature before serving. This salad is best eaten the same day it is made so the pesto does not discolor the noodles.*

*Yield:* 6 side-dish servings

### The dressing

| | |
|---|---|
| Basil Pesto | ½ cup (see page 32) |
| Light sour cream | ½ cup |
| Mayonnaise | ¼ cup |
| Lemon juice | 1 tablespoon |

### The salad

| | |
|---|---|
| Olive oil | 1 tablespoon |
| Marinated artichoke hearts | 1 6-ounce jar |
| Greek black olives, chopped | ¼ cup |
| Green onions | 3, minced |
| Fresh parsley, minced | ½ cup |
| Peas, fresh or frozen | 1 cup |
| Dried pasta | 8 ounces |

*Recommended pasta:* spirals or shells

If using frozen peas, set out to thaw ahead of time. Whisk together the dressing ingredients and set aside. Bring a large pot of water to a boil and cook the pasta until al dente. Cool in a bowl of cold water and drain well. In a large bowl, toss the pasta gently with the olive oil. Drain the artichokes, reserving their liquid for another use. Dice them and add to the pasta, along with the remaining ingredients. Toss to combine. Spoon on the dressing and toss gently but well to distribute everything evenly.

| Each serving provides: | | | |
|---|---|---|---|
| 445 | Calories | 42 g | Carbohydrate |
| 13 g | Protein | 518 mg | Sodium |
| 27 g | Fat | 17 mg | Cholesterol |

# Lentil, Feta, and Olive Pasta Salad

*We use French sheep's milk feta, which is rather dry and milder than some versions. It works beautifully with the other traditional Mediterranean foods combined in this feast of a salad. For a perfect meal, serve it with bread sticks or crunchy rolls and, of course, red wine.*

*Yield:* 8 main-course servings

### The lentils

| | | |
|---|---|---|
| Dried lentils | 1½ | cups |
| Bay leaves | 2 | |

### The dressing

| | | |
|---|---|---|
| Olive oil | ⅔ | cup |
| Red wine vinegar | ¼ | cup plus 2 tablespoons |
| Water | ¼ | cup |
| Lemon juice | ¼ | cup |
| Garlic | 2 | medium cloves, minced |
| Dried oregano | 1 | tablespoon |
| Salt | ½ | teaspoon |

### The salad

| | | |
|---|---|---|
| Dried tomatoes, slivered | ⅓ | cup |
| Calamata olives, coarsely chopped | ½ | cup |
| Green bell pepper | 1 | medium, minced |
| Feta cheese | 8 | ounces, crumbled |
| Parmesan cheese, finely grated | ½ | cup |
| Dried pasta | 12 | ounces |

*Recommended pasta:* tubes or bowties

Sort and rinse the lentils, and cover with 4 cups boiling water in a large bowl. Let sit 2–3 hours at room temperature. Drain and cook in a few cups of fresh water with the bay leaves over medium heat 10–15 minutes, until the lentils are tender but not at all mushy. Rinse with cold water to cool and refrigerate until you are ready to assemble the salad. Whisk the dressing ingredients together and set aside so the flavors can blend. Bring a pot of water to a boil and cook the pasta until al dente. Cool in a bowl of cold water and drain well. Combine the lentils, pasta, dried tomatoes, olives, bell pepper, feta, and Parmesan in a serving bowl. Toss with the dressing. Grind in a little pepper and toss again. You can allow the flavors to blend in the refrigerator for up to a few hours, but bring it to room temperature before serving. Garnish with parsley sprigs, whole olives, and dried tomato strips, if you wish.

---

Each serving provides:

| 572 | Calories | 59 g | Carbohydrate |
|------|----------|--------|--------------|
| 23 g | Protein | 654 mg | Sodium |
| 28 g | Fat | 30 mg | Cholesterol |

---

# Greek-Style Pasta Salad with Tarragon

*This salad uses the ingredients traditionally found in a Greek salad, but combines them with pasta instead of lettuce. Use black olives that are on the small side so they distribute well.*

*Yield:* 10 side-dish servings

**The dressing**

| | |
|---|---|
| Olive oil | ¼ cup |
| Garlic wine vinegar | 2 tablespoons |
| Lemon juice | 3 tablespoons |
| Dried tarragon | 1 tablespoon |

**The salad**

| | |
|---|---|
| Olive oil | 1 tablespoon |
| Whole pitted black olives | ¾ cup |
| Green olives with pimiento, sliced | ½ cup |
| Green onions | 4 minced |
| Capers, drained | 2 tablespoons |
| Feta cheese | 8 ounces, crumbled |
| Pepper | A few grinds |
| Dried pasta | 1 pound |

*Recommended pasta:* spirals or shells

Whisk together the dressing ingredients and set aside. Bring a large pot of water to a boil and cook the pasta until al dente. Cool in a bowl of cold water and drain well. In a large bowl, toss the pasta gently with 1 tablespoon olive oil, then toss with remaining ingredients until well combined. Pour the dressing over the salad and toss gently but well. Marinate at room temperature an hour or so before serving.

Each serving provides:

| 287 | Calories | 36 g | Carbohydrate |
| 8 g | Protein | 451 mg | Sodium |
| 12 g | Fat | 12 mg | Cholesterol |

# Cold Pasta with Tomatoes, Artichokes, and Capers

*This is one of our most popular creations. You must serve it someday to your favorite guests. Complete the meal with crusty garlic bread and red wine.*

*Yield:* 8 main-course servings

| | | |
|---|---|---|
| Fresh tomatoes | 1½ | pounds |
| Marinated artichoke hearts | 2 | 6-ounce jars |
| Calamata olives, chopped | ⅓ | cup |
| Capers, drained, minced if large | ¼ | cup |
| Olive oil | ⅓ | cup |
| Garlic | 3 | medium cloves, minced |
| Lemon juice | ¼ | cup |
| Red wine vinegar | 2 | tablespoons |
| Fresh oregano leaves | 2 | tablespoons |
| Salt | ¼ | teaspoon |
| Cayenne pepper | ⅛ | teaspoon |
| Feta cheese | 4 | ounces, crumbled |
| Dried pasta | 1 | pound |

*Recommended pasta:* rigatoni, penne, or other tubes

Put several quarts of water on to boil. Blanch, peel, and seed the tomatoes (see page 21). Chop coarsely and place in a large bowl. Drain the artichokes, reserving their liquid for another use. Cut them into bite-size slivers and add to the tomatoes, along with the remaining ingredients except the feta and pasta. Mix well. This can be done several hours ahead of time and can marinate, covered, at room temperature until you are ready to assemble the salad. Just before mealtime, cook the pasta until al dente in the reheated tomato-blanching water. Cool in a bowl of cold water and drain very well. Combine with the sauce and feta and toss to distribute everything evenly. Serve immediately.

---

Each serving provides:

| | | | |
|---|---|---|---|
| 393 | Calories | 51 g | Carbohydrate |
| 11 g | Protein | 615 mg | Sodium |
| 17 g | Fat | 13 mg | Cholesterol |

---

# Cold Vermicelli with Roasted Tomatoes, Fresh Basil, and Eggs

*This unusual salad has a light and refreshing effect on the palate when combined on a menu with other hot or cold dishes—at a potluck, for example. Or serve it as the main course of a light meal with crusty garlic bread and red wine.*

*Yield:* 8 side-dish servings

| | | |
|---|---|---|
| Fresh tomatoes | 1½ | pounds |
| Fresh basil leaves | 2 | cups, loosely packed |
| Garlic | 3 | medium cloves, minced |
| Olive oil | ⅔ | cup |
| Red wine vinegar | 2 | tablespoons |
| Balsamic vinegar | 2 | tablespoons |
| Salt | ½ | teaspoon |
| Pepper | | To taste |
| Eggs | 2 | large, hardboiled |
| Parmesan cheese, finely grated | ½ | cup |
| Dried pasta | 1 | pound |

*Recommended pasta:* **vermicelli or any thin strand**

Roast the tomatoes under a hot broiler. Use tongs to turn the tomatoes frequently, until they are softening and their skins have blistered, split, and charred. Set aside until they are cool enough to handle, then rub off the skins, cut in half crosswise, and squeeze out the seed pockets. Coarsely chop the tomatoes and place in a large bowl. Coarsely chop the basil and add to the tomatoes. Add the garlic, olive oil, vinegars, salt, and a few grinds of pepper. Stir well. This can be done several hours

*The Best 125 Meatless Pasta Dishes*

ahead of time and can marinate, covered, at room temperature until you are ready to assemble the salad. Just before mealtime, put several quarts of water on to boil and cook the pasta until al dente. Cool in a bowl of cold water and drain well. Cut the eggs in half lengthwise and slice each half thinly. Stir into the tomato mixture. Add the pasta to the tomato mixture, stirring and turning gently to distribute the ingredients evenly. Add the Parmesan, toss again, and serve immediately.

---

Each serving provides:

| 446 | Calories | 50 g | Carbohydrate |
| 13 g | Protein | 278 mg | Sodium |
| 22 g | Fat | 58 mg | Cholesterol |

---

# Soba Salad with Carrots, Snow Peas, and Sesame Mayo

*This pretty salad is a special treat. Do try it with earthy brown soba for an authentic Japanese flavor combination. Or use a thin green strand or ribbon. The contrast in color is an important part of the pleasure of this dish.*

*Yield:* 6 side-dish servings

**The dressing**

| | |
|---|---|
| Mayonnaise | ⅓ cup |
| Plain lowfat yogurt | ⅓ cup |
| Firm-style tofu | 2 ounces |
| Mirin or sweet sherry | 2 tablespoons |
| Soy sauce | 1 tablespoon |
| Lemon juice | 1 tablespoon |
| Fresh ginger, grated | 1 tablespoon |
| Sugar | 1 teaspoon |
| Fresh cilantro, minced | ¼ cup |
| Green onions | 2 minced |

**The salad**

| | |
|---|---|
| Snow peas | ½ pound |
| Carrot | 1 large |
| Roasted sesame oil | 1 tablespoon |
| Soy sauce | 1 tablespoon |
| Water chestnuts, sliced | ½ cup |
| Sesame seeds | 1 tablespoon |
| Lemon wedges | 1 per serving |
| Dried pasta | 8 ounces |

*Recommended pasta:* buckwheat soba, spinach linguine, or fettuccine

In a blender or food processor, puree the mayonnaise, yogurt, tofu, mirin, 1 tablespoon soy sauce, lemon juice, ginger, and sugar to a thin, smooth sauce consistency. Stir the cilantro and green onions into the dressing and set aside. This can be done several hours in advance; the flavors will blend and ripen a little over time. Store the dressing covered in the refrigerator and bring back to room temperature before tossing with the salad ingredients.

When you are ready to assemble the salad, put several quarts of water on to boil for the pasta. Pull the strings from the snow peas. Slice the carrot at a slant into very thin oblong discs. When the water is boiling, drop in the pasta and stir. For the last 2 minutes of cooking time, add the snow peas and carrots to the pot. (Remember that soba is most delicious cooked a bit beyond the al dente stage, though not until mushy.) Cool the pasta and vegetables in a bowl of cold water, drain well, and toss in a serving bowl with the sesame oil and soy sauce. Toss again with the water chestnuts and the dressing. Toast the sesame seeds (see page 20). Sprinkle the salad with the sesame seeds and garnish with lemon wedges and cilantro sprigs, if desired.

| Each serving provides: | | | |
|---|---|---|---|
| 329 | Calories | 42 g | Carbohydrate |
| 9 g | Protein | 434 mg | Sodium |
| 14 g | Fat | 8 mg | Cholesterol |

# Pasta Salad Mexicana

*Corn elbow macaroni, available in health food markets, has a wonderful texture and flavor that enhance the Mexican theme of this salad. If you can't find the corn variety, make it anyway, using another recommended pasta.*

*Yield:* 12 side-dish servings

### The dressing

| | |
|---|---|
| Avocados, very ripe | 2  large |
| Fresh cilantro, minced | ⅓ to ½ cup |
| Mayonnaise | ¼  cup |
| Plain lowfat yogurt | ¼  cup |
| Lemon juice | 3  tablespoons |
| Balsamic vinegar | 2  tablespoons |
| Soy sauce | 1  tablespoon |
| Dried oregano | 2  teaspoons |
| Chili powder | ½  teaspoon |
| Garlic powder | ½  teaspoon |

### The salad

| | |
|---|---|
| Fresh tomatoes | 2  large, coarsely chopped |
| Green bell pepper | 1  large, finely diced |
| Red cabbage, diced | ½  cup |
| Broccoli, chopped | 3  cups, loosely packed |

| | |
|---|---|
| Carrot | 1 large, diced |
| Red onion | ½ large, minced |
| Black olives, coarsely chopped | 1 cup |
| Raw sunflower seeds | ¼ cup |
| Jalapeño jack cheese | 8 ounces, grated |
| Dried pasta | 12 ounces |

*Recommended pasta:* corn elbow macaroni, spirals, or small tubes

Mix the dressing first so that the flavors have time to blend. You can whir all the dressing ingredients in a blender or food processor, or mash and whisk in a bowl to a smooth consistency. Set aside in the refrigerator. Cook the noodles until al dente. Cool in a bowl of cold water and drain well. In a large bowl, combine the fresh vegetables and the olives. Add the cooled noodles and toss. Add the dressing and combine well. Toast the sunflower seeds (see page 20). Just before serving, toss the salad again with the sunflower seeds and the cheese.

---

### Each serving provides:

| | | | |
|---|---|---|---|
| 329 | Calories | 33 g | Carbohydrate |
| 10 g | Protein | 357 mg | Sodium |
| 19 g | Fat | 23 mg | Cholesterol |

---

# Curried Pasta Salad with Currants and Almonds

*The unusual blending of sweet and savory in this salad plays delightful tricks on the palate. It is perfect served in small portions as part of a curry feast.*

*Yield:* 8 side-dish servings

### The dressing

| | | |
|---|---|---|
| Plain lowfat yogurt | ⅔ | cup |
| Half-and-half | 2 | tablespoons |
| Mirin or sweet sherry | 2 | tablespoons |
| Salt | ¼ | teaspoon |
| Curry powder | 2 | teaspoons |
| Cayenne pepper (optional) | ⅛ | teaspoon |
| Fresh cilantro, minced | ¼ | cup |
| Green onions | 3 | minced |

### The salad

| | | |
|---|---|---|
| Raw slivered almonds | ½ | cup |
| Olive oil | 1 | tablespoon |
| Currants | ½ | cup |
| Dried pasta | 8 | ounces |

*Recommended pasta:* **small shells, elbows, or tubes**

Make the dressing well ahead of time so the flavors can blend. Whisk together the yogurt, half-and-half, mirin, salt, and curry powder. Add cayenne or more curry powder if you feel the dressing needs a more spicy bite. Stir in the cilantro and green onions and set aside. When you are ready to assemble the salad, put several quarts of water on to boil for the pasta. Toast the almonds (see page 20). Cook the pasta until al dente. Cool in a bowl of cold water, drain well, and toss with the olive oil in a serving bowl. Toss the toasted almonds and the currants with the pasta, add the dressing, and toss gently to combine well. Garnish with cilantro sprigs, if you wish.

| | Each serving provides: | | |
|---|---|---|---|
| 256 | Calories | 35 g | Carbohydrate |
| 9 g | Protein | 87 mg | Sodium |
| 10 g | Fat | 3 mg | Cholesterol |

# Couscous Salad with Dried-Tomato Vinaigrette

*Though this salad has many steps, it is not difficult to prepare. The balance of sweet, smoky, and spicy is delicious.*

*Yield:* 6 side-dish servings

### The dressing

| | | |
|---|---|---|
| Olive oil | ⅓ | cup |
| Red wine vinegar | 3 | tablespoons |
| Dried oregano | 1 | teaspoon |
| Salt | ¼ | teaspoon |
| Cayenne pepper | ⅛ | teaspoon |
| Mustard seeds | 1 | tablespoon |
| Cumin seeds | 1 | tablespoon |
| Dried tomato, minced | ⅓ | cup |
| Fresh cilantro, minced | ⅓ | cup |

### The salad

| | | |
|---|---|---|
| Red bell pepper | 1 | medium |
| Water | 3 | cups |
| Salt | ¼ | teaspoon |
| Garlic powder | ¼ | teaspoon |
| Butter | 1 | tablespoon |
| Dried couscous | 2 | cups |
| Cucumber | 1 | medium, peeled, seeded |
| Red onion, minced or grated | ¼ | cup |

Well ahead of time, make the dressing so the flavors can blend. Whisk together the olive oil, vinegar, oregano, salt, and cayenne. Toast the mustard and cumin seeds together (see page 20). Stir the hot seeds into the oil mixture (they will sizzle). Add the dried tomato and cilantro. Stir, cover, and set aside at room temperature for up to several hours, until you are ready to assemble the salad. Roast the bell pepper (see page 21). Meanwhile, heat the water in a lidded saucepan until boiling. Stir in the salt, garlic powder, and butter. When butter has melted, stir in the dried couscous. Immediately cover, remove from heat, and let stand 5 minutes. Transfer couscous to a serving bowl, fluff with a fork, and set aside. Finely chop the roasted bell pepper and place in a bowl. Grate the cucumber into the bowl, add the onion and stir. Toss together the vegetables and couscous. Stir the dressing vigorously and add to the salad. Toss to distribute everything evenly.

---

Each serving provides:

| 392 | Calories | 55 g | Carbohydrate |
|---|---|---|---|
| 10 g | Protein | 217 mg | Sodium |
| 15 g | Fat | 5 mg | Cholesterol |

---

# Creamy Couscous Salad

*Serve this unusual salad as a starter course mounded on red lettuce leaves, or take it to your next picnic or family gathering. The light texture of the couscous will please everyone. You can substitute white wine vinegar if the tarragon-garlic is not available.*

*Yield:* 6 side-dish servings

### The dressing

| | | |
|---|---|---|
| Mayonnaise | ½ | cup |
| Plain lowfat yogurt | ⅓ | cup |
| Tarragon-garlic vinegar | 3 | tablespoons |
| Capers, drained and minced | 1 | heaping teaspoon |
| Garlic powder | ½ | teaspoon |
| Salt and pepper | | To taste |

### The salad

| | | |
|---|---|---|
| Olive oil | 1 | tablespoon |
| Butter | 1 | tablespoon |
| Garlic | 2 | medium cloves, minced |
| Hot water | 1½ | cups |
| Low-sodium vegetable broth cube | ½ | |
| Dried couscous | 1 | cup |
| Red bell pepper | 1 | medium, minced |
| Green bell pepper | 1 | small, minced |
| Celery | 1 | rib, minced |
| Green onions | 2 | minced |
| Fresh parsley, minced | ¾ | cup |

Blend together the dressing ingredients and refrigerate. Heat the olive oil and butter in a 2-quart saucepan. Sauté the garlic briefly, then add the water and vegetable broth cube and bring to a boil. Pour in the dried couscous. Immediately cover, remove from heat, and let stand 5 minutes. Transfer to a serving bowl, fluff with a fork, and set aside. Toss the bell peppers, celery, green onions, and parsley with the couscous until well combined. Pour on the dressing and toss again.

| Each serving provides: | | | |
|---|---|---|---|
| 310 | Calories | 29 g | Carbohydrate |
| 6 g | Protein | 179 mg | Sodium |
| 19 g | Fat | 17 mg | Cholesterol |

# Vegetable-Based Stovetop Sauces

There are many who think vegetarian cookery must be very limited and therefore boring. On the contrary! The range of textures, colors, and unique flavors found in the plant kingdom is vast and inspiring. Vegetables in all their variety are at the heart of our favorite pasta dishes. Combined with pasta, vegetables are transformed from humble side dish to main attraction.

The golden rule in vegetable cooking is to start with the very fresh. To ensure the finest quality—reassuringly free from pesticides, coloring agents, waxes, and the like—cooks can grow their own. If you have no interest in gardening, learn to recognize freshness at the market.

As with people, a radiant complexion is a sign of health in plants; brightness of color indicates freshness. Texture as well as color should be robust, so select produce that is firm, not limp and rubbery. A high water content is responsible for vegetables' refreshing crispness—dry-looking or withered produce has been too long off the plant.

The nutritious and delicious character of vegetables diminishes rapidly after harvest. Pay attention when selecting market produce—linger over the task—and the cooking will be a great pleasure, the results delectable.

While we most often prefer fresh vegetables, frozen varieties are sometimes appropriate. Specifically, frozen peas, spinach, and corn appear in a few of our recipes.

In this section, we provide some ideas for combining pasta with vegetables. May your own creativity soar.

# ✔ Burnt Garlic Pasta

*Don't let the name throw you. In this case, the garlic and butter are intentionally "burnt" to impart a special flavor.*

*Yield:* 4 side-dish servings

| | |
|---|---|
| **Butter** | 3 **tablespoons** |
| **Garlic** | 4 **medium cloves, minced** |
| **Olive oil** | 2 **tablespoons** |
| **Parmesan cheese, finely grated** | ½ **cup** |
| **Dried pasta** | 8 **ounces** |

*Recommended pasta:* **medium shells or spirals**

Put several quarts of water on to boil for the pasta. Melt the butter over high heat in a small skillet. Stir in the garlic. Turn off the heat, but continue to stir until the garlic is crisp and brown. Stir in the olive oil, then strain the mixture and discard the garlic. Cook the pasta until al dente, drain well, and transfer to a warm serving bowl. Pour the butter mixture over the pasta and toss with the Parmesan. Serve very hot.

---

### Each serving provides:

| | | | |
|---|---|---|---|
| 407 | Calories | 44 g | Carbohydrate |
| 13 g | Protein | 319 mg | Sodium |
| 20 g | Fat | 33 mg | Cholesterol |

---

# ✔ Poppy Seed Noodles

*This recipe will become one of your old favorites in no time. It is so easy to prepare, and tastes so good! Poppy seeds do lose their flavor with age, so be sure to have some fresh ones on hand. They cling nicely to curvy pasta shapes, and add a delightful crunch. This can be served as a side dish, and it also makes a wonderful light meal when accompanied by salad, bread, and cheese.*

*Yield:* 6 side-dish servings

| | | |
|---|---|---|
| **Olive oil** | 3 | **tablespoons** |
| **Garlic** | 2 | **medium cloves, minced** |
| **Salt** | ¼ | **teaspoon** |
| **Poppy seeds** | 1 | **tablespoon** |
| **Dried pasta** | 8 | **ounces** |

*Recommended pasta:* spirals or another curvy shape

Bring several quarts of water to a boil, and cook the pasta until al dente. Drain well and transfer to a warm serving bowl. Meanwhile, measure the olive oil into a tiny pan and add the garlic and salt. You do not really sauté the garlic, but simply heat it over medium heat in the oil. This takes only a moment. Pour this over the pasta and toss well to coat. Sprinkle with the poppy seeds and toss again to distribute evenly. Serve immediately.

---

### Each serving provides:

| | | | |
|---|---|---|---|
| 209 | Calories | 29 g | Carbohydrate |
| 5 g | Protein | 93 mg | Sodium |
| 8 g | Fat | 0 mg | Cholesterol |

---

# Pasta with Parsley and Sweet Roasted Garlic

*This dish is much lighter than its well-known cousin, fettuccine Alfredo. The roasted garlic adds a rich but mellow flavor. You will enjoy the results.*

*Yield:* 4 side-dish servings

| | | |
|---|---|---|
| **Garlic** | ½ | **large bulb** |
| **Olive oil** | 1 | **tablespoon plus ½ teaspoon** |
| **Light sour cream** | ⅓ | **cup** |
| **Half-and-half** | ¼ | **cup** |
| **Fresh parsley, minced** | ½ | **cup** |
| **Dry sherry** | 2 | **tablespoons** |
| **Dried pasta** | 8 | **ounces** |

*Recommended pasta:* **fettuccine or lasagnette**

Preheat oven or toaster oven to 400 degrees F. Cut ¼ inch off the garlic bulb to barely expose the tops of the cloves. Do not peel. Drizzle on about ½ teaspoon olive oil and bake about 30–45 minutes. Bring several quarts of water to a boil for the pasta. When the garlic bulb is very soft, remove it from the oven and cool. Remove the garlic from the skin by squeezing the cloves from the bottom. The garlic will slide out of the cut end as a soft paste. Whisk the garlic paste with the sour cream, light cream, parsley, and sherry in a small saucepan. Stir and cook over very low heat until just heated through. Meanwhile, cook the pasta until al dente, drain well, and toss with 1 tablespoon olive oil in a warm serving bowl. Quickly reheat the garlic sauce, if necessary, toss with the noodles, and serve.

---

Each serving provides:

| 342 | Calories | 55 g | Carbohydrate |
| 11 g | Protein | 44 mg | Sodium |
| 8 g | Fat | 6 mg | Cholesterol |

---

# ✔ Dried-Tomato Carbonara

*Dried tomatoes have a meaty texture and smoky flavor that might even fool your favorite carnivore. For this dish, use dried tomatoes that have been reconstituted in olive oil. You can also use the oil from the tomatoes where olive oil is called for in this recipe.*

*Yield:* 6 side-dish servings

| | | |
|---|---|---|
| Oil-packed dried tomatoes, drained, slivered | ½ | cup |
| Eggs | 2 | large, beaten |
| Olive oil | ⅓ | cup |
| Garlic | 2 | medium cloves, minced |
| Red wine vinegar | 1 | tablespoon |
| Madeira | 2 | tablespoons |
| Parmesan cheese, finely grated | ½ | cup |
| Black olives, finely chopped | ½ | cup |
| Dried pasta | 12 | ounces |

*Recommended pasta:* fettuccine or tagliarini

Drain as much oil as possible from the tomatoes before slivering. Bring several quarts of water to a boil and cook the pasta until al dente. Meanwhile, in a large bowl, stir together the eggs, olive oil, garlic, red wine vinegar, Madeira, and Parmesan. Quickly but thoroughly drain the cooked pasta and transfer to a warmed serving bowl. Immediately pour the egg mixture over the very hot pasta.° Lift and toss to distribute everything evenly. Add the olives and toss again. Serve immediately, passing the pepper grinder and additional Parmesan, if desired.

Each serving provides:

| | | | |
|---|---|---|---|
| 451 | Calories | 49 g | Carbohydrate |
| 14 g | Protein | 284 mg | Sodium |
| 22 g | Fat | 77 mg | Cholesterol |

°Due to the controversy concerning raw eggs and salmonella bacteria, add eggs when pasta is very hot, *not* warm. For further information, contact your local office of the U.S. Department of Agriculture.

# ✔ Pasta with Kasseri and Pine Nuts

*It is wonderful to live with a man who likes to cook. Guy Hadler created this simple dish one night when there was "nothing to eat." Another of his creative successes was born.*

*Yield:* 6 side-dish servings

| | |
|---|---|
| Pine nuts | ½ cup |
| Olive oil | 2 tablespoons |
| Kasseri or Parmesan cheese, finely grated | ⅓ cup |
| Dried pasta | 12 ounces |

*Recommended pasta:* **bowties or spirals**

Bring several quarts of water to a boil and cook the pasta until al dente. Meanwhile, toast the pine nuts (see page 20). Drain the pasta well and toss with the pine nuts, olive oil, and cheese in a warm bowl. Serve immediately.

---

### Each serving provides:

| | | | |
|---|---|---|---|
| 336 | Calories | 44 g | Carbohydrate |
| 12 g | Protein | 104 mg | Sodium |
| 13 g | Fat | 4 mg | Cholesterol |

---

# ✔ Pasta with Cilantro Pesto and Avocado

*The cilantro gives this dish a delightful south-of-the-border flavor. Serve it on a summer evening with salsa, chips, and margaritas.*

*Yield:* 4 main-course servings

| | |
|---|---|
| Raw pumpkin seeds | ¼ cup |
| Cilantro Pesto | 1¼ cups (see page 34) |
| Light sour cream | ½ cup |
| Red bell pepper | 1 medium, minced |
| Avocado, firmly ripe | 1 sliced |
| Dried pasta | 12 ounces |

*Recommended pasta:* **medium shells, spirals, or tubes**

Bring several quarts of water to a boil and cook the pasta until al dente. Drain well and transfer to a warm serving bowl. Meanwhile, toast the pumpkin seeds (see page 20) and mince. Stir together the Cilantro Pesto and sour cream. Heat briefly over very low heat. Toss the hot noodles with bell pepper. Add the pesto mixture and toss again. Serve with the avocado slices and minced pumpkin seeds on top.

---

Each serving provides:

| | | | |
|---|---|---|---|
| 600 | Calories | 82 g | Carbohydrate |
| 16 g | Protein | 70 mg | Sodium |
| 24 g | Fat | 0 mg | Cholesterol |

---

# Pasta with Many Peppers
# and Almonds

*Make this dish in late summer, when peppers are at their best. The colors satisfy the senses nearly as much as the flavors do.*

*Yield:* 4 main-course servings

| | | |
|---|---|---|
| Yellow bell pepper | 1 | large |
| Red bell pepper | 1 | large |
| Fresh Anaheim chilies | 2 | large |
| Butter | 2 | tablespoons |
| Dried red chili flakes | ½ | teaspoon |
| Garlic | 3 | medium cloves, minced |
| Red onion | 1 | medium, coarsely chopped |
| Whole blanched unsalted almonds | ½ | cup |
| Salt | ¼ | teaspoon |
| Pepper | | A few grinds |
| Dried oregano | 1 | teaspoon |
| Fresh parsley, minced | ¼ | cup, firmly packed |
| Dry sherry | ½ | cup |
| Parmesan cheese, finely grated | ⅓ | cup |
| Dried pasta | 8 | ounces |

*Recommended pasta:* linguine, fettuccine, or any long ribbon variety

Put several quarts of water on to boil. Cut bell peppers lengthwise into quarters. Remove the seeds and pith and slice across each section to create uniform ¼-inch strips. Halve the

Anaheim peppers lengthwise, remove seeds and pith, and slice crosswise into uniform ¼-inch strips. Melt the butter in a large skillet, add the chili flakes and garlic, and stir a moment before adding the peppers, onion, almonds, salt, and pepper. Stir and toss a minute or two over medium-high heat. The peppers should sizzle and fry in the butter. As the peppers begin to release their liquid you may leave the pan, but continue to stir frequently as they sauté 10 minutes. Meanwhile, cook the pasta until al dente. When peppers are a little limp and well browned, sprinkle on the oregano, turn off the heat, and add the parsley and sherry. Stir the peppers as the liquid sizzles and steams. Toss this mixture with hot, drained noodles, grind on a little more pepper, and garnish the bowl or platter with parsley sprigs. Sprinkle with Parmesan and serve.

| Each serving provides: | | | |
|---|---|---|---|
| 479 | Calories | 59 g | Carbohydrate |
| 15 g | Protein | 359 mg | Sodium |
| 18 g | Fat | 22 mg | Cholesterol |

# ✔ Pizza Pasta

*Here, favorite pizza toppings become a quick and delicious sauce for pasta. For best results, use fontina or another good melting cheese.*

*Yield:* 6 main-course servings

| | | |
|---|---|---|
| **Olive oil** | 4 | tablespoons |
| **Onion** | 1 | medium, chopped |
| **Green bell pepper** | 1 | small, chopped |
| **Garlic** | 2 | medium cloves, minced |
| **Mushrooms, chopped** | 2 | cups |
| **Black olives, coarsely chopped** | 1 | cup |
| **Fresh tomatoes** | 1 | pound, chopped |
| **Dried basil** | 1 | teaspoon |
| **Dried oregano** | 1 | teaspoon |
| **Dried thyme** | | A pinch |
| **Cayenne pepper** | | A few shakes |
| **Dry red wine** | ¼ | cup |
| **Fontina cheese, grated** | 1 | cup |
| **Parmesan cheese, finely grated** | ¼ | cup |
| **Dried pasta** | 12 | ounces |

*Recommended pasta:* **spirals, tubes, or shells**

Put several quarts of water on to boil for the pasta. Heat 2 tablespoons of the olive oil in a skillet. Add the onion, bell pepper, and garlic, and sauté over medium heat about 5 minutes. Add the mushrooms, olives, tomatoes, herbs, cayenne, and wine and simmer, uncovered, about 10 minutes. The vegetables should release their juices and cook down just a bit. Meanwhile, cook the pasta until al dente. Drain briefly. Toss the hot noodles in a warm bowl with the remaining 2 tablespoons olive oil and the cheeses, then toss in the vegetable mixture. Serve very hot and pass the pepper grinder, if desired.

---

Each serving provides:

| 444 | Calories | 51 g | Carbohydrate |
|-----|----------|------|--------------|
| 15 g | Protein | 435 mg | Sodium |
| 20 g | Fat | 25 mg | Cholesterol |

---

# Spicy Stir-Fried Tofu
and Green Beans

*This hearty meal in a dish is a delicious and unusual way to enjoy
fresh beans.*

*Yield:* 8 main-course servings

| | | |
|---|---|---|
| Fresh green beans | 1 | pound |
| Firm-style tofu | 1 | pound |
| Olive oil | 3 | tablespoons |
| Dried red chili flakes | ½ | teaspoon |
| Onion | 1 | medium, coarsely chopped |
| Garlic | 4 | medium cloves, minced |
| Soy sauce | 5 | tablespoons |
| Red bell pepper | 1 | small, diced |
| Mushrooms | ½ | pound, sliced |
| Mirin or sweet sherry | 3 | tablespoons |
| Lemon juice | 2 | tablespoons |
| Dried pasta | 1 | pound |

*Recommended pasta:* **spaghetti or linguine**

Trim the green beans and break or cut into 1-inch pieces. Blot
the tofu with a tea towel to remove surface water and dice into
½-inch cubes. Put several quarts of water on to boil for the
pasta. Heat the olive oil in a high-walled heavy skillet. Add the
chili flakes and stir to distribute. Add the onion and garlic and
sauté over medium-high heat, stirring often, 5 minutes. Add
1 tablespoon of the soy sauce and stir to distribute before adding the tofu, bell pepper, and mushrooms. The pan should be
hot enough so that the tofu begins to sizzle immediately. Sauté,

stirring frequently, about 8 minutes, until the liquid released from the tofu is gone and everything is browning. Bring a few inches of water to a boil in a covered pot, insert a steaming rack, and steam the beans 8 minutes. Drain and add to the tofu mixture. Stir and sauté 5 minutes longer. Meanwhile, cook the pasta until al dente. Drain well and transfer to a warm serving bowl. Add the tofu mixture to the pasta and toss. Whisk together the remaining 3 tablespoons soy sauce, the mirin, and the lemon juice in a small bowl. Pour this mixture over the pasta, toss to combine well, and serve very hot.

---

Each serving provides:

| 390 | Calories | 55 g | Carbohydrate |
|-----|----------|------|--------------|
| 19 g | Protein | 660 mg | Sodium |
| 11 g | Fat | 0 mg | Cholesterol |

---

# Pasta with Pesto, Potatoes, and Green Beans

*"Potatoes with pasta?" you ask. Yes, this combination works very well. The green beans add a nice light crunch.*

*Yield:* 4 main-course servings

| | | |
|---|---|---|
| **Olive oil** | 1 | tablespoon |
| **Garlic** | 2 | medium cloves, minced |
| **Stewed tomatoes** | 1 | 14.5-ounce can |
| **Fresh green beans** | ½ | pound |
| **Red potato** | 1 | medium |
| **Basil Pesto** | ½ | cup (see page 32) |
| **Half-and-half** | ½ | cup |
| **Dried pasta** | 12 | ounces |

*Recommended pasta:* **penne or other small tubes**

Heat the oil in a large high-walled skillet and sauté the garlic a few moments. Add tomatoes and cook over medium-high heat about 12 minutes to reduce the liquid. Meanwhile, trim the green beans and cut into 1-inch pieces. Dice the potato into

½-inch cubes. Put a couple of inches of water into a lidded pot, insert a steamer tray, and bring to a boil. Steam the beans and potato together until tender-crisp, about 6 minutes. Meanwhile, bring several quarts of water to a boil for the pasta. When the sauce is reduced, stir in the pesto and half-and-half. Heat through. Cook the pasta until al dente; drain well. Toss in a warm bowl with the steamed vegetables and sauce. Serve immediately.

---

### Each serving provides:

| | | | |
|---|---|---|---|
| 632 | Calories | 90 g | Carbohydrate |
| 21 g | Protein | 469 mg | Sodium |
| 23 g | Fat | 18 mg | Cholesterol |

---

# Stewed Cauliflower and Potato with Cumin

*The vegetables stew until they're soft and blend together to create a wonderfully aromatic topping for pasta.*

*Yield:* 6 main-course servings

| | | |
|---|---|---|
| Butter | 3 | tablespoons |
| Cauliflower | 1 | medium, chopped |
| Russet potato | 1 | medium, diced |
| Onion | 1 | medium, chopped |
| Cumin seeds | 1 | tablespoon |
| Garlic | 2 | medium cloves, minced |
| Salt | ½ | teaspoon |
| Pepper | | A few grinds |
| Tomato juice | ½ | cup |
| Dry sherry | ½ | cup |
| Water | 1 | cup |
| Dried oregano | 2 | teaspoons |
| Black olives, coarsely chopped | ½ | cup |
| Fresh cilantro, minced | ¼ | cup |
| Cheddar or jalapeño jack cheese, grated | 1 | cup |
| Dried pasta | 1 | pound |

*Recommended pasta:* sturdy tubes or spirals

Put several quarts of water on to boil for the pasta. Melt the butter in a high-walled skillet and add the cauliflower, potato, onion, cumin, garlic, salt, and pepper. Sauté over medium heat, stirring frequently, 15 minutes. Add the tomato juice, sherry, water, and oregano and bring to a simmer. Reduce heat

*The Best 125 Meatless Pasta Dishes*

to low, cover, and simmer 15 minutes. Vegetables will be very soft. Meanwhile, cook the pasta until al dente. Toss the drained hot noodles with the stewed vegetables in a warm bowl, then toss again with the olives, cilantro, and cheese. Serve very hot.

---

Each serving provides:

| | | | |
|---|---|---|---|
| 500 | Calories | 70 g | Carbohydrate |
| 17 g | Protein | 548 mg | Sodium |
| 15 g | Fat | 35 mg | Cholesterol |

---

# Sweet and Sour Eggplant Sauce

*This slightly spicy sauce is one of our favorite ways to eat eggplant, especially served on buckwheat soba, which has a unique earthy flavor. Try it as a main course for a large group of friends.*

*Yield:* 10 main-course servings

| | | |
|---|---|---|
| Sesame seeds | 3 | tablespoons |
| Roasted sesame oil | 2 | tablespoons |
| Onion | 1 | medium, chopped |
| Garlic | 3 | medium cloves, minced |
| Dried red chili flakes | ½ | teaspoon |
| Eggplants | 2 | medium (about 2 pounds), chopped |
| Yellow or red bell peppers | 2 | medium, chopped |
| Tomato puree | ½ | cup |
| Ground ginger | 1½ | teaspoons |
| Soy sauce | 3 | tablespoons |
| Cider vinegar | 3 | tablespoons |
| Honey | 3 | tablespoons |
| Arrowroot powder | 1 | tablespoon |
| Fresh cilantro, minced | ½ | cup |
| Dried pasta | 1½ | pounds |

*Recommended pasta:* buckwheat soba or linguine

Toast the sesame seeds (see page 20) and set aside. Heat the oil and 2 tablespoons water in a high-walled skillet and sauté the onion, garlic, and chili flakes a few moments. Stir in the eggplant and bell peppers. Sauté over low heat about 20 minutes, stirring frequently. The vegetables should become limp but not extremely soft. Meanwhile, bring several quarts of water to a boil. Whisk together 1½ cups water, the tomato puree, ginger, and soy sauce. Add to the skillet and simmer, covered, 10 minutes. Cook pasta until al dente and drain well. (If using buckwheat soba, cook a bit past the al dente stage—until fairly soft, but not mushy.) Whisk the vinegar, honey, and arrowroot powder together in a small bowl. Add the vinegar mixture to the vegetables, turn off heat, and stir and turn a few moments until sauce thickens. Make a bed of the pasta on a platter or in a shallow bowl, arrange eggplant sauce on top, and sprinkle with cilantro and sesame seeds. Serve very hot.

Each serving provides:

| 351 | Calories | 66 g | Carbohydrate |
| 11 g | Protein | 368 mg | Sodium |
| 5 g | Fat | 0 mg | Cholesterol |

*Vegetable-Based Stovetop Sauces*

# Carrots and Artichoke Hearts with Pistachios and Feta

*The delicate but distinctive flavors of the individual ingredients blend well in this Greek-inspired feast.*

*Yield:* 6 main-course servings

| | | |
|---|---|---|
| Carrots | 2 | medium |
| Water-packed artichoke bottoms | 1 | 14-ounce can, drained |
| Shelled whole pistachios | ½ | cup |
| Olive oil | 4 | tablespoons |
| Red onion | 1 | large, coarsely chopped |
| Garlic | 2 | medium cloves, minced |
| Dried red chili flakes | ½ | teaspoon |
| Fresh parsley, minced | ¼ | cup, firmly packed |
| Lemon juice | 2 | tablespoons |
| Water | ¼ | cup |
| Feta cheese | 4 | ounces, crumbled |
| Lemon wedges | 1 | per serving |
| Dried pasta | 12 | ounces |

*Recommended pasta:* mostaccioli, penne, or spirals

Slice the carrots on the diagonal into ⅛-inch discs. Chop the artichoke bottoms into bite-size wedges. Remove as much of the pistachios' papery skin as you can and toast them (see page 20). Mince the pistachios and set aside. Put several quarts of water on to boil for the pasta. Heat 2 tablespoons of the olive oil in a large skillet. Add the carrots, onion, garlic, and chili flakes and sauté over medium heat about 10 minutes, stirring frequently. Add the artichoke bottoms and parsley and sauté, stirring occasionally, 5 minutes longer. Stir in the lemon juice and water and immediately turn off the heat. Meanwhile, cook the pasta until al dente and drain briefly. In a warm serving dish, toss the hot noodles with the remaining 2 tablespoons olive oil, the feta, and pistachios. Add the sautéed vegetables and toss again. Serve hot with lemon wedges.

| | Each serving provides: | | |
|---|---|---|---|
| 452 | Calories | 57 g | Carbohydrate |
| 15 g | Protein | 253 mg | Sodium |
| 19 g | Fat | 17 mg | Cholesterol |

# Mediterranean Asparagus and Artichokes

*This was inspired by a day when glorious sunshine fooled us into thinking it was spring. We began to dream of the Mediterranean Sea and invented this dish to take us there in spirit.*

*Yield:* 6 main-course servings

| | | |
|---|---|---|
| Asparagus | 1½ | pounds |
| Marinated artichoke hearts | 1 | 15-ounce jar |
| Olive oil | 4 | tablespoons |
| Onion | 1 | medium, coarsely chopped |
| Garlic | 4 | medium cloves, minced |
| Dried oregano | 2 | teaspoons |
| Dried spearmint | 2 | teaspoons |
| Salt | ¼ | teaspoon |
| Pepper | | A few grinds |
| Dried tomatoes, slivered | ½ | cup |
| White wine | ¾ | cup |
| Parmesan cheese, finely grated | ½ | cup |
| Fresh parsley, minced | ¼ | cup |
| Dried pasta | 1 | pound |

*Recommended pasta:* **sturdy tubes or spirals**

Put several quarts of water on to boil for the pasta. Break off the tough stem ends of the asparagus and cut at a slant into 1-inch pieces. Drain the artichoke hearts, reserving the liquid for another use. Heat 2 tablespoons of the olive oil in a large skillet. Sauté the onion and garlic with the oregano and spearmint 5 minutes, until the onion is golden and limp. Add the aspar-

agus, salt, and pepper; stir and sauté 5 minutes. Add the artichoke hearts and dried tomatoes; stir and sauté 5 minutes
longer. Meanwhile, cook the pasta until al dente. Drain well.
Stir the wine into the asparagus mixture and immediately turn
off the heat. In a warm serving bowl, toss the hot drained noodles with the remaining 2 tablespoons olive oil and the Parmesan. Toss again with the vegetable mixture. Sprinkle with the
minced parsley and serve.

| Each serving provides: | | | |
|---|---|---|---|
| 492 | Calories | 70 g | Carbohydrate |
| 18 g | Protein | 302 mg | Sodium |
| 14 g | Fat | 6 mg | Cholesterol |

# Grilled Vegetables in Dried-Tomato Marinade

*This dish is best prepared during the summer when you can use the barbecue. The flavors are wonderful, as is the presentation—perfect for an outdoor dinner party. You can grill and marinate the vegetables before your guests arrive, if you wish.*

*Yield:* 6 main-course servings

### The marinade

| | |
|---|---|
| Olive oil | ⅓ cup |
| Balsamic vinegar | 2 tablespoons |
| Lemon juice | 1 tablespoon |
| Garlic | 4 medium cloves, minced |
| Fresh basil leaves, minced | ¼ cup |
| Fresh parsley, minced | ½ cup |
| Fresh thyme leaves, minced | 1 tablespoon |
| Dried tomatoes, chopped | ¾ cup |
| Salt and pepper | To taste |

### The vegetables

| | |
|---|---|
| Red onions | 2 medium |
| Zucchini or crookneck squash | 4 small |
| Japanese eggplants | 4 small |
| Belgian endive | 2 heads |
| Olive oil | 2 tablespoons |
| Parmesan cheese, finely grated | ¾ cup |
| Dried pasta | 1 pound |

*Recommended pasta:* spirals or spaghetti

*The Best 125 Meatless Pasta Dishes*

The marinade can be made ahead, or just before dinnertime. Whisk together the olive oil, vinegar, and lemon juice until light and slightly creamy in appearance. Add the garlic, basil, parsley, thyme, and dried tomatoes. Stir to combine. Add salt and pepper if desired. Set aside at room temperature.

Heat the grill. Cut the red onions into ½-inch slices. Cut the squash lengthwise into quarters. Halve the eggplants lengthwise. Leave the stem end intact on the endive, but slice it lengthwise and fan it out. Place the vegetables on a large platter and brush them lightly with the olive oil. Since the onions have the longest cooking time and are the least delicate of all the vegetables, place them on the hottest part of the grill. Cook them about 3 minutes, then turn them and continue to cook. Next, place the squash on the grill, then the eggplant and endive. Turn after about 2 minutes. When all the vegetables are tender, transfer them to a large bowl. Allow them to cool slightly, then cut them into small pieces. Pour the marinade over the vegetables and toss well to combine. Marinate about 1 hour at room temperature. When you are ready to serve dinner, bring several quarts of water to a boil and cook the pasta until al dente. Drain well and combine with the vegetables. Toss well to coat with the marinade and to distribute the vegetables throughout. Serve at once, passing the Parmesan.

Each serving provides:

| 571 | Calories | 77 g | Carbohydrate |
|---|---|---|---|
| 19 g | Protein | 260 mg | Sodium |
| 22 g | Fat | 10 mg | Cholesterol |

# Summer Squash with Fresh Basil and Madeira

*At the height of summer, pick young squash and mature basil to create this light and refreshing dish. If you combine green zucchini or scallop squash with yellow crookneck, the colors will interplay very nicely on the plate.*

*Yield:* 6 main-course servings

| | | |
|---|---|---|
| **Olive oil** | 3 | tablespoons |
| **Onions** | 2 | medium, chopped |
| **Garlic** | 3 | medium cloves, minced |
| **Summer squash** | 1½ | pounds, coarsely chopped |
| **Salt** | ½ | teaspoon |
| **Cayenne pepper** | ⅛ | teaspoon |
| **Fresh basil leaves** | 2 | cups, loosely packed |
| **Madeira** | ½ | cup |
| **Parmesan cheese, finely grated** | ½ | cup |
| **Eggs** | 2 | large |
| **Lemon wedges** | 1 | per serving |
| **Dried pasta** | 12 | ounces |

*Recommended pasta:* **spaghetti or linguine**

Heat 2 tablespoons of the olive oil in a heavy skillet over medium heat. Sauté the onion and garlic about 3 minutes, until onion is barely translucent. Add the squash, salt, and cayenne pepper; stir and sauté 5 minutes longer. Add 2 tablespoons water, cover tightly, and cook over low heat about 10 minutes.

*The Best 125 Meatless Pasta Dishes*

The squash should be crisp-tender. Add the basil. Stir a moment or two, until the basil begins to wilt. Add the Madeira, bring to a simmer, and turn off the heat. Meanwhile, bring several quarts of water to a boil and cook the pasta until al dente. Drain well. Toss in a warm serving bowl with the Parmesan. Add the squash mixture and toss again. Lightly beat the eggs and add to the bowl, lifting and turning the pasta to distribute the egg evenly.* Act quickly so the eggs do not cook, but rather are incorporated into the sauce. Serve very hot with lemon wedges and additional Parmesan, if you wish.

---

### Each serving provides:

| | | | |
|---|---|---|---|
| 413 | Calories | 57 g | Carbohydrate |
| 15 g | Protein | 366 mg | Sodium |
| 12 g | Fat | 77 mg | Cholesterol |

---

*Due to the controversy concerning raw eggs and salmonella bacteria, add eggs when the sauce is very hot, *not* warm. For further information, contact your local office of the U.S. Department of Agriculture.

# Spinach and Eggplant with Dried Tomato and Feta

*Cooking the fresh spinach separately and very briefly retains its bright flavor, which is an important part of the pleasure of this dish. Wait to try this until you find spinach at the market that is absolutely beautiful.*

*Yield:* 6 main-course servings

| | | |
|---|---|---|
| Fresh spinach | 1 | bunch (about ¾ pound) |
| Eggplant | 2 | small (about 1½ pounds) |
| Olive oil | 5 | tablespoons |
| Garlic | 3 | medium cloves, minced |
| Dried rosemary | 1 | teaspoon |
| Salt | ½ | teaspoon |
| Dried tomatoes, slivered | ¼ | cup, loosely packed |
| Capers, drained, minced | 1 | tablespoon |
| Parmesan cheese, finely grated | ½ | cup |
| Feta cheese | 8 | ounces, crumbled |
| Lemon juice | 2 | tablespoons |
| Pepper | | Several grinds |
| Lemon wedges | 1 | per serving |
| Dried pasta | 12 | ounces |

*Recommended pasta:* vermicelli or linguine

Put a few cups of water on to boil in your pasta pot. Carefully wash the spinach and discard stems. When the water is boiling, drop the spinach into the pot all at once. Cook 2 minutes, or

*The Best 125 Meatless Pasta Dishes*

until spinach wilts. Use a skimmer to lift the spinach out of the pot. Cool in a bowl of cold water and use your hands to squeeze out almost all the liquid. Coarsely chop the spinach and set aside. Add a few quarts of water to the spinach cooking liquid and bring to a boil for the pasta. Without peeling, coarsely chop the eggplant. Heat 3 tablespoons of the olive oil in a wok or large skillet. Add the garlic and rosemary, stir and sauté a minute, then add the eggplant and salt. Quickly stir and toss to coat with seasonings. Sauté over medium heat 15 minutes, stirring frequently. It will soften considerably. Add the tomatoes, capers, and chopped spinach, stir to combine, cover, and turn off heat. Cook the pasta until al dente, drain it briefly, then toss in a warm serving bowl with the remaining 2 tablespoons olive oil, the Parmesan, feta, and lemon juice. Add the eggplant mixture, grind in some pepper, and toss again. Serve very hot or at room temperature with lemon wedges and additional Parmesan, if desired.

---

Each serving provides:

| 502 | Calories | 57 g | Carbohydrate |
|---|---|---|---|
| 19 g | Protein | 840 mg | Sodium |
| 23 g | Fat | 40 mg | Cholesterol |

---

# Spicy Brussels Sprouts with Baby Corn and Shiitake

*This dish packs a hefty wallop on the spicy scale, thanks to a generous quantity of dried red chili flakes. You can reduce the amount, if you wish, or wait to make it until you're in the mood for hot food.*

*Yield:* 6 main-course servings

| | | |
|---|---|---|
| Dried shiitake mushrooms | 1 | ounce |
| Sesame seeds | 2 | tablespoons |
| Raw sunflower seeds | ¼ | cup |
| Brussels sprouts | 1 | pound |
| Carrot | 1 | large |
| Roasted sesame oil | 3 | tablespoons |
| Garlic | 3 | medium cloves, minced |
| Dried red chili flakes | 1 | teaspoon |
| Onion | 1 | large, coarsely chopped |
| Salt | ¼ | teaspoon |
| Soy sauce | 3 | tablespoons |
| Water-packed baby corn | 1 | 15-ounce can, drained |
| Arrowroot powder | 1 | tablespoon |
| Dried pasta | 1 | pound |

*Recommended pasta:* linguine or vermicelli

Soak the mushrooms in 3 cups hot water 30–45 minutes. Lift them from the water, squeeze out excess water, and wash carefully under a thin stream of running water to remove any grit lodged in the layers of membrane under the caps. Cut out and discard the tough stems and sliver the caps. Set aside. Strain the mushroom soaking liquid through a paper coffee filter and set aside. Toast the sesame and sunflower seeds separately (see page 20). Combine the toasted seeds and set aside. Put several quarts of water on to boil for the pasta. Trim outer leaves from the brussels sprouts. If they are tiny, cut them in half. Quarter the larger ones. Cut the carrot into thick 2-inch-long matchsticks. Heat the oil in a heavy high-walled skillet and sauté the garlic and chili flakes for a few moments before adding the brussels sprouts, carrot, and onion. Add the salt. Stir and sauté over medium heat 10–15 minutes, until vegetables are browned and tender. Meanwhile, cook the pasta until al dente. Add the mushroom soaking liquid and soy sauce to the vegetable mixture, then stir in the corn and mushrooms. Heat to simmering. Meanwhile, whisk the arrowroot powder with ⅓ cup cold water. Add all at once to the simmering skillet and stir to distribute. Cook 30 seconds. The sauce will thicken slightly. Toss the hot sauce with the drained pasta in a warmed serving bowl. Garnish with toasted seeds.

---

Each serving provides:

| | | | |
|---|---|---|---|
| 481 | Calories | 77 g | Carbohydrate |
| 17 g | Protein | 641 mg | Sodium |
| 13 g | Fat | 0 mg | Cholesterol |

---

# Hot Baba Ghanoush with Pasta

*Why not take a favorite Middle Eastern eggplant and tahini dish, usually served as an appetizer, and toss it with noodles to make a complete meal? The results are delicious. Make the sauce several hours before dinnertime so the flavors can blend.*

*Yield:* 6 main-course servings

| | |
|---|---|
| **Eggplant** | 1 medium (about 1 pound) |
| **Plain lowfat yogurt** | ½ cup |
| **Tahini (sesame butter)** | ¼ cup |
| **Dry sherry** | ¼ cup |
| **Lemon juice** | ¼ cup |
| **Garlic** | 3 medium cloves, minced |
| **Olive oil** | 3 tablespoons |
| **Salt** | ½ teaspoon |
| **Cayenne pepper** | ⅛ teaspoon |
| **Parmesan cheese, finely grated** | ⅓ cup |
| **Fresh parsley, minced** | ¼ cup |
| **Dried pasta** | 1 pound |

*Recommended pasta:* spirals or wide ribbons

Heat the oven to 400 degrees F. Pierce the eggplant with a fork in several places and bake in a glass baking dish 40–50 minutes, until it is totally soft and ready to collapse. Prod it with a fork to tell when it is done. Meanwhile, whisk together the yogurt, tahini, sherry, lemon juice, garlic, 2 tablespoons of the olive oil, the salt, and cayenne. Set aside. When eggplant is soft, remove from the oven. When it is cool enough to handle, remove the skin and scoop the flesh into the yogurt mixture. Whip with a fork until homogenous. This much can be done several hours, or even a day or two, in advance. Cover the mixture and refrigerate until you are ready for it.

Bring several quarts of water to a boil and cook the pasta until al dente. Drain well. Meanwhile, heat the eggplant mixture over low heat on top of the stove just to warm it a bit. Toss the hot, drained noodles with the remaining 1 tablespoon olive oil and the Parmesan. When well combined, add the eggplant mixture and toss again to distribute evenly. Garnish with minced parsley. Serve hot or at room temperature.

---

Each serving provides:

| 473 | Calories | 67 g | Carbohydrate |
| 15 g | Protein | 319 mg | Sodium |
| 15 g | Fat | 5 mg | Cholesterol |

---

# Tempeh and Veggies with Miso Tahini Sauce

*Typically, rich and chunky sauces combine best with a substantial noodle like rigatoni or spirals. But in this case—maybe because of the light touch of lemon—humble spaghetti is the best choice. For a super-quick and simple meal, use lightly steamed instead of sautéed vegetables.*

*Yield:* 6 main-course servings

| | | |
|---|---|---|
| Japanese eggplants | 2 | medium |
| Tempeh | 8 | ounces |
| Olive oil | 2 | tablespoons |
| Garlic | 3 | medium cloves, minced |
| Dried red chili flakes | ½ | teaspoon |
| Onion | 1 | medium, coarsely chopped |
| Red bell pepper | 1 | small, slivered |
| Dried oregano | 2 | teaspoons |
| Salt | ½ | teaspoon |
| Lemon juice | ½ | cup |
| Water | ¾ | cup |
| Miso | 2 | tablespoons |
| Tahini (sesame butter) | ½ | cup |
| Dry sherry | 2 | tablespoons |
| Soy sauce | 1 | tablespoon |
| Carrots | 2 | medium, thinly sliced |
| Cauliflower florets | 2 | cups |
| Broccoli florets | 2 | cups |

| Lemon wedges | 1 | per serving |
| Dried pasta | 1 | pound |

*Recommended pasta:* spaghetti or linguine

Without peeling them, thickly slice the eggplants crosswise at a slant. Dice the tempeh. Put several quarts of water on to boil. Heat the olive oil in a heavy high-walled skillet. Sauté the garlic and chili flakes a moment or two, then add the eggplant, tempeh, onion, and bell pepper. Stir in the oregano and salt. Sauté over medium-high heat 15 minutes, stirring very frequently. The vegetables should brown and fry a bit and become very tender. Set aside.

Combine the lemon juice with the water. With a wooden spoon, mash the miso and tahini together in a small saucepan until homogenous. Pour in about a quarter of the lemon water and whisk to incorporate. Add the remaining lemon water, the sherry, and the soy sauce and whisk briskly until very smooth. The sauce will be thin. Heat this mixture over low heat until hot, but do not simmer. Cook the pasta until al dente, adding the carrots, cauliflower, and broccoli to the pot for the last 4 minutes of cooking time. Drain the pasta and vegetables. Combine in a warm bowl with the miso tahini sauce and top with the sautéed vegetables. Serve very hot with lemon wedges.

---

### Each serving provides:

| 599 | Calories | 84 g | Carbohydrate |
| 25 g | Protein | 628 mg | Sodium |
| 20 g | Fat | 0 mg | Cholesterol |

---

# ✔ Broccoli-Mushroom Satay

*This dish will surprise you with many new flavors. It is easy to prepare and pretty to serve. Stir-fry sauce is a pungent mixture available at Asian markets or gourmet food shops.*

*Yield:* 4 main-course servings

| | | |
|---|---|---|
| Roasted sesame oil | 2 | tablespoons |
| Green onions | 5, | thinly sliced |
| Red bell pepper | 1 | medium, diced |
| Green bell pepper | 1 | small, diced |
| Garlic | 4 | medium cloves, minced |
| Fresh ginger, grated | 1 | tablespoon |
| Water | ½ | cup |
| Stir-fry sauce | 2 | tablespoons |
| Rice wine vinegar | 1 | tablespoon |
| Soy sauce | 2 | tablespoons |
| Creamy peanut butter | 2 | tablespoons |
| Broccoli, coarsely chopped | 2½ | cups |
| Mushrooms | ½ | pound, thickly sliced |
| Light sour cream | ½ | cup |
| Fresh Chinese noodles | 14 | ounces |

*Alternate pasta:* **fresh fettuccine or linguine**

Heat the oil gently in a wok or large cast-iron skillet. Add the green onions, bell peppers, garlic, and ginger. Sauté over low heat about 5 minutes, stirring often. Pour in the water, the stir-fry sauce, vinegar, and soy sauce. Whisk in the peanut butter. Add the broccoli and mushrooms and increase the heat. Cover and cook over medium heat about 10 minutes; uncover, stir, and continue to cook 5 minutes. Meanwhile, cook the Chinese noodles a bit past the al dente stage—until fairly soft, but not mushy. Stay close to the pot, as fresh noodles cook quickly. (If using a standard pasta variety, cook until al dente.) Drain and transfer them to a warm serving bowl. Turn off the heat under the sauce, add the sour cream, and stir gently. Pour the sauce over the noodles and serve immediately.

| Each serving provides: | | | |
|---|---|---|---|
| 377 | Calories | 59 g | Carbohydrate |
| 15 g | Protein | 528 mg | Sodium |
| 10 g | Fat | 7 mg | Cholesterol |

# Sesame Soba with Burdock Root and Carrot

*Rick and Cathy Tokubo inspired this dish. For the most authentic results, use one of the Asian noodle varieties—particularly buckwheat soba. Burdock root is available at Asian markets. Pick up the soba, sesame oil, and the mirin while you are there.*

*Yield:* 4 side-dish servings

| | | |
|---|---|---|
| Burdock root | 1 | root (about ¼ pound) |
| Carrot | 1 | large |
| Olive oil | 1 | tablespoon |
| Roasted sesame oil | 1 | tablespoon |
| Dried red chili flakes | ½ | teaspoon |
| Fresh ginger, grated | 1 | tablespoon |
| Green onions | 2, | thinly sliced |
| Mung bean sprouts | 1 | cup |
| Soy sauce | 3 | teaspoons |
| Light sour cream | ⅓ | cup |
| Mirin or sweet sherry | 1 | tablespoon |
| Sesame seeds | 1 | tablespoon |
| Lemon wedges | 1 | per serving |
| Soba | 8 | ounces |

*Alternate noodle:* **any thin Asian variety**

Peel the burdock root, shaving off only the thinnest layer of skin. Have a bowl of ice water standing by. Cut the root into 3-inch sections, then cut each section into slender matchsticks. As you finish cutting each section, drop the slivers into the ice water to minimize darkening. Leave them there until you need them. Cut the carrot into matchsticks about the same size as the burdock. Add to the ice water. Put several quarts of water on to boil for the noodles. Heat the oils and chili flakes in a heavy skillet a moment. Drain the carrot and burdock and blot them dry with a tea towel, then sauté in the oil over medium-high heat 10 minutes, stirring frequently. They will begin to brown. Add the ginger, green onions, bean sprouts, and 2 teaspoons of the soy sauce. Stir and sauté another 10 minutes while you cook the noodles a bit past the al dente stage until fairly soft, but not mushy. Meanwhile, whisk the sour cream with the mirin and the remaining teaspoon of soy sauce. Set aside. Toast the sesame seeds (see page 20). When the noodles are cooked, drain briefly and toss with the sour cream sauce, then with the vegetable mixture. Serve with lemon wedges in a bowl or on a platter, hot or at room temperature, sprinkled with the toasted sesame seeds.

Each serving provides:

| 361 | Calories | 57 g | Carbohydrate |
| 11 g | Protein | 300 mg | Sodium |
| 10 g | Fat | 0 mg | Cholesterol |

# Spicy Greens with Adzuki Beans and Shiitake

*Adzukis are tiny, red, protein-packed beans from the Orient. They are available in most Asian markets and natural food stores. For a Far East feast, begin the meal with a very simple miso broth and end with tea and almond cookies.*

*Yield:* 6 main-course servings

| | |
|---|---|
| Dried adzuki beans | 1 cup |
| Dried red chili flakes | 1 teaspoon |
| Bay leaves | 2 |
| Dried shiitake mushrooms | 1 ounce |
| Hot water | 2 cups |
| Mustard greens | 2 bunches (about 1½ pounds) |
| Roasted sesame oil | 2 tablespoons |
| Garlic | 3 medium cloves, minced |
| Onion | 1 medium, diced |
| Fresh ginger, grated | 2 tablespoons |
| Soy sauce | 2 tablespoons |
| Dried pasta | 1 pound |

*Recommended pasta:* linguine or lasagnette

Soak the beans several hours or overnight. Drain and cover with fresh water in a large stockpot. Add the chili flakes and bay leaves. Bring to a boil and cook, adding water occasionally as needed, 40 minutes. Beans should be tender but not so soft they break apart easily. Drain the beans and set aside.

Meanwhile, soak the mushrooms in the hot water about 45 minutes. Lift them out of the water, reserving the soaking liquid, and wash carefully under a thin stream of running water to remove any grit in the membranes. Remove the tough stems and sliver the caps. Drain the soaking liquid through a paper coffee filter into a bowl. You will have about 1½ cups, which you will use in the sauce. Set aside.

Wash the greens carefully, discard the thick part of the stems, and chop coarsely. Bring several quarts of water to a boil and cook the pasta until al dente. Meanwhile, in a high-walled skillet or stockpot, heat the oil and sauté the garlic and onion about 5 minutes, until the onion begins to get limp. Add the beans, ginger, and soy sauce, and stir and sauté 5 minutes longer. Add the greens and the mushroom soaking liquid. Toss and stir often as the greens steam and most of the liquid evaporates, about 10 minutes. Gently combine the sauce with the hot noodles in a warm serving bowl. Pass the pepper grinder and additional soy sauce, if desired.

---

Each serving provides:

| 484 | Calories | 89 g | Carbohydrate |
|---|---|---|---|
| 20 g | Protein | 378 mg | Sodium |
| 6 g | Fat | 0 mg | Cholesterol |

---

# Tomato-Based Stovetop Sauces

Tomatoes and pasta are made for each other. When raw or barely cooked, this summer fruit yields a delicate sweetness that perfectly complements pasta's hearty substance. When cooked for a long time, tomatoes are transformed to a thick and rich paste which can stand alone as a sauce or can carry any number of other ingredients.

Many of our recipes call for fresh pear tomatoes. Sometimes called Italian plum or Roma tomatoes, they are small, oblong fruits that have fewer seeds and less juice than salad-variety tomatoes. Their meatier texture reduces quickly to a thick sauce consistency when cooked.

The very best tomatoes are homegrown. Once you have tasted just-picked tomatoes, still warm with the sun, you will understand the difference between truly fresh produce and that which is sold as "fresh" at the supermarket! Tomatoes are simple to grow in areas where the summers are dependably warm and there is ample water for their cultivation.

If you are unable or unwilling to grow tomatoes, seek out a brand of canned tomatoes with a sweet, full-bodied flavor. Stock up on canned whole tomatoes, stewed tomatoes, tomato puree, tomato paste, and pear tomatoes. They will come in handy time after time. Canned tomatoes are not always an appropriate substitute in recipes that call for fresh, but we have offered you the option in several cases.

In this section we explore some of the infinite possibilities suggested by the classic combination of tomato and pasta. We hope they will inspire your own culinary adventures.

# Fresh Salsa

*We begin this chapter with a simple fresh salsa recipe that can be used in recipes where fresh salsa is called for. If you live in a region where fresh salsa is available from the supermarket, you may want to use the commercial variety instead.*

*Yield:* 5 cups

| | | |
|---|---|---|
| Fresh tomatoes | 2½ | pounds |
| Whole green chilies | 1 | 7-ounce can |
| Fresh lemon juice | ¼ | cup |
| Onion | 1 | medium, finely diced |
| Fresh cilantro, minced | ⅓ | cup |
| Garlic | 3 | cloves, minced |
| Salt | ⅛ | teaspoon |
| Black pepper | | A few grinds |

Blanch and peel the tomatoes (see page 21). Coarsely chop them, drain off as much juice as possible, and set aside in a bowl. Drain the liquid from the canned green chilies. Finely chop them and add to the tomatoes. Add the lemon juice to the tomato mixture, along with the onion, cilantro, garlic, salt, and pepper. Though its flavor improves over time, this salsa can be enjoyed immediately with corn chips or as a topping for Mexican-style dishes. Store the portion you don't need right away in a tightly closed container in the refrigerator for several days, or freeze it for longer periods. If you are accustomed to canning foods, this recipe may be made in larger quantities and put up for the pantry.

Each ½ cup portion provides:

| 32 | Calories | 8 g | Carbohydrate |
|----|----------|-----|--------------|
| 1 g | Protein | 158 mg | Sodium |
| 0 g | Fat | 0 mg | Cholesterol |

# Quick and Simple Tomato Coulis

*Over the years, you will come up with many tasty variations on this basic theme. If you are having a lot of company, double or triple the amount of tomatoes, garlic, and herbs to increase the yield.*

*Yield:* 4 side-dish servings

| | | |
|---|---|---|
| Fresh pear tomatoes (or 1 28-ounce can whole tomatoes) | 3 | pounds |
| Olive oil | 1 | tablespoon |
| Garlic | 2 | medium cloves, minced |
| Herbs, fresh or dried | | Amounts vary |
| Salt | ½ | teaspoon |
| Pepper | | A few grinds |
| Parmesan or other dry cheese (optional), grated | ½ | cup |
| Dried pasta | 12 | ounces |

*Recommended pasta:* simple strands like spaghetti or vermicelli are traditional with a simple tomato sauce, but you can experiment

Bring several quarts of water to a boil. Blanch, peel, and seed the tomatoes (see page 21), and chop coarsely. If using canned tomatoes, drain off the juice and reserve for another use, such as soup. Heat the oil in a heavy-bottomed skillet and stir and sauté the garlic about a minute, then pour in the tomatoes all at once. Cook over medium-high heat, stirring frequently, about 5 minutes. The tomatoes will break apart and liquefy a bit. Add a tablespoon or so of fresh oregano or basil leaves, or a smaller amount of fresh rosemary or thyme. Any combination of the above is quite appropriate, and delicious. If using dried herbs, begin with a teaspoon or so of oregano and/or basil, perhaps

*The Best 125 Meatless Pasta Dishes*

¼ teaspoon of the stronger-flavored thyme and rosemary. Salt and pepper the sauce at this stage, using the recommended amounts as a rule of thumb, but varying to your own taste. Simmer only a few minutes more over medium-high heat, until the liquid has reduced considerably. You'll know by the look of it when you've achieved the right consistency. The starch from the cooked pasta will thicken the sauce a bit when they are combined, so it's all right for the sauce to appear a bit thin. Meanwhile, cook the pasta until al dente in the reheated tomato-blanching water. In a warmed bowl, toss the tomato sauce with hot pasta and the cheese, if desired. You can pass more cheese at the table. Alternately, you can toss the cooked noodles with a bit of olive oil, portion them out onto serving plates, and top with a ladleful of sauce, sprinkling cheese on top.

*Variations:* When adding the herbs, you can include a tablespoon or two of capers or chopped olives. A few ounces of red wine, sherry, or brandy can be added for a distinctive effect. In place of plain herbs, you can stir in a few tablespoons of prepared herbal pesto (see pages 31–36). Let your imagination take you for a ride and experiment fearlessly. You might make a delicious mistake!

---

### Each serving provides:

| | | | |
|---|---|---|---|
| 419 | Calories | 80 g | Carbohydrate |
| 14 g | Protein | 310 mg | Sodium |
| 6 g | Fat | 0 mg | Cholesterol |

---

# Tomato Sauce with Fresh Oregano

*Simple tomato sauces can be used in many different recipes. This one has a very fresh, light flavor that works well over noodles or in a baked dish.*

*Yield:* 6 side-dish servings

| | | |
|---|---|---|
| Olive oil | 2 | tablespoons |
| Garlic | 3 | medium cloves, minced |
| Whole tomatoes | 2 | 28-ounce cans |
| Bay leaves | 3 | |
| Fresh oregano leaves | ¼ | cup |
| Lemon | 2 | thin slices |
| Dried pasta | 1 | pound |

*Recommended pasta:* **spaghetti, linguine, or rigatoni**

Heat the olive oil in a large pan and gently sauté the garlic a few seconds. Add the tomatoes, along with their juice, the bay leaves, oregano, and lemon slices. Cook over medium-high heat about 45 minutes, stirring frequently so the tomatoes do not scorch. The mixture should reduce to a sauce consistency. Meanwhile, bring several quarts of water to a boil and cook the pasta until al dente. Remove the bay leaves and lemon slices from the sauce and serve over pasta, or use in other recipes that call for basic tomato sauce.

---

Each serving provides:

| | | | |
|---|---|---|---|
| 381 | Calories | 70 g | Carbohydrate |
| 12 g | Protein | 437 mg | Sodium |
| 6 g | Fat | 0 mg | Cholesterol |

---

# ✔ Tomato Pesto Pasta

*The pesto gives this tomato sauce a new twist.*

*Yield:* 6 main-course servings

| | | |
|---|---|---|
| Olive oil | 2 | tablespoons |
| Garlic | 2 | medium cloves, minced |
| Stewed tomatoes | 2 | 14.5-ounce cans |
| Basil Pesto | 1 | cup (see page 32) |
| Dried pasta | 12 | ounces |

*Recommended pasta:* vermicelli, spaghetti, or tagliarini

Heat the olive oil in a skillet and sauté the garlic a minute or two. Add the tomatoes and simmer over medium-high heat until liquid is greatly reduced, about 15 minutes. Meanwhile, bring several quarts of water to a boil and cook the pasta until al dente. Drain well and transfer to a warm bowl. Stir the pesto into the tomato mixture and heat through. Toss with the pasta and serve.

---

### Each serving provides:

| | | | |
|---|---|---|---|
| 513 | Calories | 61 g | Carbohydrate |
| 17 g | Protein | 572 mg | Sodium |
| 25 g | Fat | 10 mg | Cholesterol |

---

# Vegetable Ragout

*A good old standby spaghetti sauce—even the carnivores in your family will love it. You can halve or double the quantities for fewer or more diners. Or make a double batch and freeze in quart jars—some hectic evening you'll be glad you stocked up.*

*Yield:* 10 main-course servings

| | | |
|---|---|---|
| Olive oil | 2 | tablespoons |
| Onion | 1 | large, chopped |
| Garlic | 4 | medium cloves, minced |
| Green bell pepper | 1 | large, diced |
| Dried red chili flakes | 1 | teaspoon |
| Dried rosemary | 1 | teaspoon |
| Mushrooms | ½ | pound, chopped |
| Zucchini | 2 | medium, grated |
| Dried basil | 1 | tablespoon |
| Dried oregano | 1 | tablespoon |
| Salt | ½ | teaspoon |
| Whole tomatoes | 1 | 28-ounce can |
| Tomato puree | 1 | 28-ounce can |
| Bay leaves | 2 | |
| Red wine | ½ | cup |
| Parmesan cheese, finely grated | ½ | cup |
| Dried pasta | 2 | pounds |

*Recommended pasta:* spaghetti or vermicelli

Heat the olive oil in a high-walled, heavy skillet. Add the onion, garlic, bell pepper, chili flakes, and rosemary. Stir and sauté over medium heat 5 minutes. Add the mushrooms, zucchini, basil, oregano, and salt. Stir and sauté 3 minutes. When

*The Best 125 Meatless Pasta Dishes*

the vegetables just begin to release their juices, add the tomatoes, tomato puree, and bay leaves. Bring to a simmer. Reduce heat to low and cook uncovered 20 minutes, stirring frequently. While sauce is cooking, bring several quarts of water to a boil. Cook the pasta until al dente and drain well. Meanwhile, add the wine to the sauce and simmer about 10 minutes. Toss the sauce with the hot pasta and Parmesan. Pass additional Parmesan at the table, if you wish.

Each serving provides:

| | | | |
|---|---|---|---|
| 464 | Calories | 85 g | Carbohydrate |
| 17 g | Protein | 656 mg | Sodium |
| 6 g | Fat | 4 mg | Cholesterol |

# ✔ Angel Hair with Tomatoes and Fresh Basil

*This light, refreshing dish is best made in the summer with tomatoes and basil from the garden. However, with fresh basil available in many supermarkets year round, this dish can be prepared in the winter with canned tomatoes. Be sure to heat the serving bowls and the individual bowls or plates. The angel hair pasta is so delicate that it loses its heat rapidly when served in a cold bowl.*

*Yield:* 4 side-dish servings

| | | |
|---|---|---|
| Fresh pear tomatoes (or 1 14.5-ounce can whole tomatoes) | 1½ | pounds |
| Olive oil | 2 | tablespoons |
| Garlic | 3 | medium cloves, minced |
| Fresh basil leaves, chopped | 1 | cup, loosely packed |
| Parmesan cheese, finely grated (optional) | ½ | cup |
| Dried angel hair pasta | 8 | ounces |

*Recommended pasta:* if angel hair (cappellini) is unavailable, substitute vermicelli or thin tagliarini

Bring several quarts of water to a boil. Blanch, peel, and seed the tomatoes (see page 21) and chop coarsely. If using canned tomatoes, drain off the juice and reserve for another use, such as soup. Heat the oil in a large skillet and sauté the garlic a few moments. Add the tomatoes, bring to a rapid simmer, then cook over medium-high heat about 10 minutes, until the tomato liquid is reduced and beginning to thicken. Stir frequently during the last 5 minutes of cooking to prevent scorching. Meanwhile, cook the pasta in the reheated tomato-blanching water until al dente. Drain and transfer to a warm bowl. Add the basil to the tomato sauce and stir to distribute. Pour over the pasta, toss, and serve immediately. Pass the Parmesan, if desired.

| Each serving provides: | | | |
|---|---|---|---|
| 315 | Calories | 53 g | Carbohydrate |
| 9 g | Protein | 18 mg | Sodium |
| 8 g | Fat | 0 mg | Cholesterol |

# ✔ Pasta Oliveto

*You must use the very best fresh tomatoes for this dish, so wait until summertime to make it. Served hot or at room temperature, it is a light but quite satisfying summer luncheon or supper. Crusty French rolls and a crisp green salad would be the perfect accompaniments.*

*Yield:* 6 main-course servings

| | | |
|---|---|---|
| Fresh tomatoes | 3 | pounds |
| Salt | ½ | teaspoon |
| Red wine vinegar | 3 | tablespoons |
| Pepper | | A few grinds |
| Whole pitted black olives | 1½ | cups |
| Olive oil | ⅓ | cup plus 2 tablespoons |
| Garlic | 3 | medium cloves, chopped |
| Parmesan cheese, finely grated | ½ | cup |
| Dried pasta | 1 | pound |

*Recommended pasta:* **spaghettini, tagliarini, or vermicelli**

Bring several quarts of water to a boil. Blanch, peel, and seed the tomatoes (see page 21) and coarsely chop. In a large bowl, toss the tomatoes with the salt, vinegar, and pepper. Set aside. Drain the olives. In a food processor, puree the olives with the ⅓ cup olive oil and the chopped garlic. Meanwhile, cook the pasta until al dente in the reheated tomato-blanching water. If you wish to serve the dish at room temperature, cool the noodles in a bowl of cold water, drain, and toss with 2 tablespoons of the olive oil. If serving the dish hot, drain the noodles. Toss the hot or cool noodles, first with the olive paste, then with the tomatoes, until everything is well combined. Serve hot or at room temperature and pass the Parmesan and the pepper grinder.

---

Each serving provides:

| 535 | Calories | 66 g | Carbohydrate |
|------|----------|------|--------------|
| 15 g | Protein | 646 mg | Sodium |
| 24 g | Fat | 6 mg | Cholesterol |

---

# ✔ Light Tomato Cream with Pesto

*Pesto and tomatoes, all dressed up! What a pretty presentation this makes when served on an elegant plate garnished with fresh basil and lemon slices.*

*Yield:* 4 main-course servings

| | | |
|---|---|---|
| Fresh pear tomatoes | 2 | pounds |
| Olive oil | 1 | tablespoon |
| Garlic | 2 | medium cloves, minced |
| Capers, drained, minced | 2 | tablespoons |
| Basil Pesto | ¼ | cup (see page 32) |
| Plain nonfat yogurt | ¼ | cup |
| Half-and-half | 2 | tablespoons |
| Pine nuts | ¼ | cup |
| Parmesan cheese, finely grated | ½ | cup |
| Dried pasta | 12 | ounces |

*Recommended pasta:* bowties or fancy shells

Bring several quarts of water to a boil. Blanch, peel, and seed the tomatoes (see page 21). Chop coarsely. Heat the olive oil in a skillet and sauté the garlic a few moments. Add the tomatoes and simmer over medium-high heat until most of the liquid has been reduced, about 10 minutes. Add the capers, turn off the heat, and cover to keep warm. In a small saucepan, blend together the pesto, sour cream, and half-and-half. Set aside. Meanwhile, cook the pasta until al dente in the reheated tomato-blanching water, drain, and transfer to a warm serving bowl. Toast the pine nuts (see page 20). In a small saucepan, blend together the pesto, yogurt, and half-and-half. Gently heat the pesto mixture over very low heat. When it is quite warm, toss with the hot noodles. Top with the tomatoes and pine nuts. Serve at once, passing the Parmesan.

---

Each serving provides:

| 590 | Calories | 81 g | Carbohydrate |
| 23 g | Protein | 424 mg | Sodium |
| 21 g | Fat | 15 mg | Cholesterol |

---

# ✔ Tomato Sauce with Tarragon and Capers

*This sauce is lightly cooked to retain the tangy flavors of pickled capers and fresh tarragon.*

*Yield:* 6 main-course servings

| | | |
|---|---|---|
| Whole tomatoes | 1 | 28-ounce can |
| Tomato paste | ⅓ | cup |
| Capers, drained | ⅓ | cup |
| Fresh tarragon leaves | ¼ | cup, lightly packed |
| Salt | ¼ | teaspoon |
| Olive oil | 1 | tablespoon |
| Garlic | 3 | medium cloves, minced |
| Romano cheese, finely grated | ½ | cup |
| Dried pasta | 1 | pound |

*Recommended pasta:* **spaghettini, tagliarini, or vermicelli**

Drain the tomatoes, and save the juice for another use, such as soup. In a blender or food processor, puree the tomatoes, tomato paste, capers, tarragon, and salt. Put several quarts of water on to boil for the pasta. Heat the olive oil in a heavy skillet and sauté the garlic a minute or two. Add the tomato mixture and cook over low heat 10–15 minutes or so, until very hot but not simmering. Meanwhile, cook the pasta until al dente and drain well. Toss with the sauce in a warm bowl. Serve hot with a sprinkling of Romano cheese.

| Each serving provides: | | | |
|---|---|---|---|
| 379 | Calories | 66 g | Carbohydrate |
| 14 g | Protein | 678 mg | Sodium |
| 7 g | Fat | 9 mg | Cholesterol |

# Tomatoes with Sweet Rosemary Onions

*Braising in butter mellows the onions to a delectable sweetness which is complemented by the earthy flavor of dried rosemary. Crumble the rosemary between your palms before adding, so it is well distributed throughout the sauce.*

*Yield:* 6 side-dish servings

| | | |
|---|---|---|
| **Butter** | 2 | **tablespoons** |
| **Olive oil** | 2 | **tablespoons** |
| **Onions** | 3 | **large, coarsely chopped** |
| **Dried rosemary** | 1½ | **teaspoons** |
| **Salt** | ½ | **teaspoon** |
| **Fresh pear tomatoes** | 4 | **pounds** |
| **Pepper** | | **A few grinds** |
| **Dried pasta** | 1 | **pound** |

*Recommended pasta:* **linguine or fettuccine**

*The Best 125 Meatless Pasta Dishes*

Heat the butter and olive oil in a heavy skillet. Sauté the onions with the rosemary and ¼ teaspoon of the salt over low heat 30 minutes, stirring occasionally. Bring several quarts of water to a boil. Blanch, peel, and seed the tomatoes (see page 21) and chop coarsely. Add the tomatoes and the remaining ¼ teaspoon salt to the onions. Bring to a rapid simmer over medium-high heat, then reduce to low and simmer gently another 20 minutes, stirring frequently. Meanwhile, cook the pasta until al dente in the reheated tomato-blanching water. Drain. Toss with the sauce in a warm bowl and grind a little pepper on top before serving.

Each serving provides:

| 435 | Calories | 75 g | Carbohydrate |
|---|---|---|---|
| 13 g | Protein | 250 mg | Sodium |
| 10 g | Fat | 10 mg | Cholesterol |

# ✔ Angel Hair with Tomatoes and Fresh Shiitake

*The delicate strands of angel hair pasta provide the perfect bed for this tomato mushroom sauce. Though light, this dish is very filling. Fresh shiitake are available in well-stocked gourmet food shops.*

*Yield:* 4 side-dish servings

| | | |
|---|---|---|
| Stewed tomatoes | 1 | 14.5-ounce can |
| Olive oil | 2 | tablespoons |
| Garlic | 3 | medium cloves, minced |
| Onion | 1 | medium, finely diced |
| Yellow bell pepper | 1 | medium, finely diced |
| Dry red wine | ½ | cup |
| Fresh shiitake mushrooms | 4 | ounces, coarsely chopped |
| Fresh oregano leaves | 1 | tablespoon |
| Dried pasta | 8 | ounces |

*Recommended pasta:* angel hair (cappellini), vermicelli, or thin tagliarini

Drain the tomatoes, reserving their liquid, and dice. Heat the olive oil in a skillet and gently sauté the garlic, onion, and bell pepper about 2 minutes. Add the wine, mushrooms, oregano, and the tomatoes with their juice. Bring to a rapid simmer over medium-high heat and cook about 5 minutes. Turn down the heat and simmer gently about 6 more minutes. Meanwhile, cook the pasta until al dente. Drain well and transfer to a warm serving bowl. Top with the sauce and serve very hot.

---

Each serving provides:

| 321 | Calories | 54 g | Carbohydrate |
|------|----------|--------|-------------|
| 9 g | Protein | 269 mg | Sodium |
| 8 g | Fat | 0 mg | Cholesterol |

---

# ✔ Pasta Primavera

*This dish uses ingredients straight from your summer garden; however, any grocery store will also have what you need any time of the year.*

*Yield:* 6 main-course servings

| | | |
|---|---|---|
| Onion | 1 | large |
| Eggplant, peeled, diced | 2 | cups |
| Zucchini | 2 | medium, diced |
| Yellow bell pepper | 1 | medium, coarsely chopped |
| Fresh tomatoes | 2 | large, coarsely chopped |
| Garlic | 3 | medium cloves, minced |
| Tomato juice | 1½ | cups |
| Fresh basil leaves, minced | ½ | cup |
| Half-and-half | ¼ | cup |
| Parmesan cheese, finely grated | ½ | cup |
| Dried pasta | 12 | ounces |

*Recommended pasta:* **fettuccine or linguine**

Cut the onion in half lengthwise and slice the halves. Combine with the eggplant, zucchini, bell pepper, tomatoes, and garlic in a large cast-iron skillet. Add the tomato juice and bring to a gentle simmer over medium heat. Cover and cook about 10 minutes. Uncover, add the basil, and cook several more minutes to reduce the liquid. The vegetables should be tender but not too soft. Meanwhile, bring several quarts of water to a boil and cook the pasta until al dente. Drain. Just before serving, gently stir the half-and-half into the vegetable mixture. Spoon the vegetable mixture over the noodles on a warm platter and serve immediately. Pass the Parmesan.

| Each serving provides: | | | |
|---|---|---|---|
| 314 | Calories | 55 g | Carbohydrate |
| 13 g | Protein | 388 mg | Sodium |
| 5 g | Fat | 10 mg | Cholesterol |

# Spicy Tomato Sauce with Arugula and Calamata Olives

*This dish is a nice blending of unusual ingredients. As a variation, you could use fresh chopped spinach in place of the arugula.*

*Yield:* 6 side-dish servings

| | | |
|---|---|---|
| Fresh pear tomatoes (or 1 28-ounce can) | 3 | pounds |
| Olive oil | 2 | tablespoons |
| Garlic | 2 | medium cloves, minced |
| Dried red chili flakes | ½ | teaspoon |
| Calamata olives, chopped | ½ | cup |
| Arugula, chopped | 2 | cups |
| Parmesan cheese, finely grated | 1 | cup |
| Dried pasta | 12 | ounces |

*Recommended pasta:* rigatoni or penne

If you are using fresh tomatoes, bring several quarts of water to a boil. Blanch, peel, and seed the tomatoes (see page 21) and chop coarsely. If using canned tomatoes, drain them and reserve juice for another use, such as soup. Heat the olive oil over low heat in a large cast-iron skillet. Add the garlic and chili flakes and sauté a minute or two. Add the tomatoes and olives, increase the heat, and simmer about 10 minutes, until the sauce is reduced. Cook the pasta until al dente in the reheated tomato-blanching water, drain well, and toss with the arugula in a warm serving bowl. Pour the tomato sauce over and toss to combine. Serve immediately, passing the Parmesan.

---

Each serving provides:

| | | | |
|---|---|---|---|
| 364 | Calories | 50 g | Carbohydrate |
| 16 g | Protein | 420 mg | Sodium |
| 12 g | Fat | 13 mg | Cholesterol |

---

# Spicy Tomato Cauliflower Sauce

*This dish makes a hearty cold-weather meal and looks beautifully rich on a plate.*

*Yield:* 8 main-course servings

| | | |
|---|---|---|
| Olive oil | 2 | tablespoons |
| Onion | 1 | medium, coarsely chopped |
| Green bell pepper | 1 | medium, coarsely chopped |
| Garlic | 4 | medium cloves, minced |
| Dried red chili flakes | 1 | teaspoon |
| Cauliflower | 1 | medium |
| Salt | ½ | teaspoon |
| Tomato puree | 1 | 28-ounce can |
| Dried oregano | 1 | tablespoon |
| Water | ½ | cup |
| Dry sherry | ½ | cup |
| Romano cheese, finely grated | ½ | cup |
| Fresh cilantro, minced | ¼ | cup |
| Dried pasta | 1 | pound |

*Recommended pasta:* rigatoni or other hearty tubes

Heat the oil in a high-walled skillet and sauté the onion, bell pepper, garlic, and chili flakes over medium-high heat 5 minutes, stirring frequently. Meanwhile, cut the cauliflower into medium florets. Add the cauliflower and salt to the sautéed vegetables and toss to combine. Add the tomato puree, oregano, and the water. Cook over medium-high heat until the sauce begins to bubble, then turn the heat to low, cover, and simmer 30 minutes. Just before serving, stir in the sherry and heat through. Meanwhile, bring several quarts of water to a boil and cook the pasta until al dente; drain. Toss with the sauce in a warm bowl, then toss again with Romano and cilantro. Serve very hot and pass the pepper grinder and additional grated cheese, if you wish.

Each serving provides:

| 342 | Calories | 58 g | Carbohydrate |
|------|----------|--------|--------------|
| 12 g | Protein | 604 mg | Sodium |
| 6 g | Fat | 5 mg | Cholesterol |

# Tex-Mex Tofu and Noodles

*This is a substantial dish—serve only a tart and leafy salad to finish the meal. This recipe calls for fresh homemade salsa. However, you may substitute commercially prepared fresh salsa, bearing in mind the sodium content will be higher.*

*Yield:* 8 main-course servings

| | | |
|---|---|---|
| Fresh homemade salsa | 1½ | cups |
| Fresh corn (or 1 10-ounce package frozen) | 3 | medium ears |
| Firm-style tofu | 1 | pound |
| Chard | 1 | bunch (about ¾ pound) |
| Whole pitted black olives | 1½ | cups |
| Olive oil | 2 | tablespoons |
| Red onion | 1 | medium, coarsely chopped |
| Garlic | 2 | medium cloves, minced |
| Chili powder | 1 | teaspoon |
| Dried oregano | 1 | teaspoon |
| Whole tomatoes | 1 | 14.5-ounce can |
| Light sour cream | 1 | cup |
| Cheddar or jack cheese, finely grated | ½ | cup |
| Fresh cilantro, minced | ½ | cup |
| Dried pasta | 1 | pound |

**Recommended pasta:** rigatoni, spirals, or penne

Prepare fresh salsa (see page 172). Set aside. If using frozen corn, set out to thaw well ahead of time. If using fresh corn, cut

*The Best 125 Meatless Pasta Dishes*

the kernels from the cob and set aside. Blot the tofu to remove surface water and dice into bite-size cubes. Wash the chard and remove the stems. Sliver the stems and coarsely chop or tear the leaves. Drain the olives and quarter lengthwise. Put several quarts of water on to boil for the pasta. Heat the oil in a high-walled skillet, and sauté the onion and garlic over medium-high heat about 5 minutes, or until they are limp. Stir in the chili powder and oregano, then immediately add the tofu. Stir and sauté another 5 minutes. Add the corn and chard, and sauté until greens are wilted and almost all the moisture is gone, about 5 minutes. Meanwhile, whir the salsa and tomatoes together in a blender for a few moments to create a thick puree. Stir into the tofu mixture, along with the olives, and heat gently 5 more minutes. Turn off the heat and add the sour cream and cheese to the sauce. Stir until the cheese melts and the sauce is well blended. Meanwhile, cook the pasta until al dente and drain well. Toss in a warm bowl with the sauce and serve piping hot with the cilantro sprinkled on top.

---

Each serving provides:

| 478 | Calories | 65 g | Carbohydrate |
|---|---|---|---|
| 23 g | Protein | 480 mg | Sodium |
| 16 g | Fat | 7 mg | Cholesterol |

---

# Tomato Madeira Sauce with Avocado

*The dense and rather mysterious flavor of this sauce is enlivened by the addition of ripe raw avocado just before serving. Grilled fish would be a good accompaniment.*

*Yield:* 6 side-dish servings

| | | |
|---|---|---|
| Fresh tomatoes | 1½ | pounds |
| Avocado, firmly ripe | 1 | medium |
| Lemon juice | 2 | tablespoons |
| Onion | 1 | medium |
| Whole pitted black olives | 1½ | cups |
| Whole green chilies | 1 | 3.5-ounce can |
| Olive oil | ¼ | cup |
| Dried oregano | 1 | teaspoon |
| Cumin seeds | 1 | teaspoon |
| Chili powder | ½ | teaspoon |
| Dried rosemary | ½ | teaspoon |
| Garlic | 4 | medium cloves, minced |
| Madeira | ½ | cup |
| Salt | ½ | teaspoon |
| Cayenne pepper | ¼ | teaspoon |
| Parmesan cheese, finely grated | ½ | cup |
| Dried pasta | 12 | ounces |

*Recommended pasta:* medium tubes or spirals

Bring several quarts of water to a boil. Blanch, peel, and seed the tomatoes (see page 21) and chop coarsely. Meanwhile, cut the avocado in half, remove the pit and peel, and dice the flesh into a small bowl. Toss with the lemon juice and set aside. Cut the onion in half lengthwise, then slice each half thickly. Drain the olives and quarter them. Clean any seeds and membranes out of the chilies and slice them into long narrow strips. Heat the olive oil in a large heavy skillet, add the oregano, cumin seeds, chili powder, and rosemary and stir for a moment to distribute evenly in the oil. Add the onion and garlic and sauté, stirring frequently, 7–8 minutes, until onion begins to get limp. Add the tomatoes, olives, chilies, Madeira, salt, and cayenne. Simmer over medium heat 15 minutes. The sauce will thicken and reduce considerably. Meanwhile, cook the pasta until al dente in the reheated tomato-blanching water. Drain thoroughly, toss in a serving bowl with hot sauce and Parmesan, then very gently with avocado in lemon juice. Serve immediately, passing more cheese if you wish.

---

### Each serving provides:

| | | | |
|---|---|---|---|
| 453 | Calories | 55 g | Carbohydrate |
| 12 g | Protein | 624 mg | Sodium |
| 20 g | Fat | 5 mg | Cholesterol |

---

# Pasta with Peppers and Tomatoes

*This sauce is a beautiful bright red, yet not dominated by a tomato flavor. The red bell peppers add sweetness and the chilies a bit of fire. Make this dish at the end of the summer when the ingredients are the freshest.*

*Yield:* 6 main-course servings

| | | |
|---|---|---|
| Fresh Anaheim chilies | 16 | medium |
| Fresh pear tomatoes | 5-6 | pounds |
| Olive oil | ⅓ | cup |
| Red bell peppers | 4 | large, coarsely chopped |
| Garlic | 7 | medium cloves, minced |
| Salt and pepper | | To taste |
| Dried pasta | 1 | pound |

*Recommended pasta:* linguine or lasagnette

Roast, peel, and seed the chilies (see page 21); if you enjoy very spicy food, leave some or all of the seeds. Cut the chilies into long, thin strips. When working with these mild chilies, you needn't wear gloves; however, be careful not to rub your eyes, as the pepper juice will burn them. Wash your hands with soap and hot water when you finish. Bring several quarts of water to a boil. Blanch, peel, and seed the tomatoes (see page 21) and chop coarsely. Heat the olive oil over low heat in a large cast-iron skillet. Add the chilies and bell peppers, stirring gently to distribute them evenly in the pan. Cook over medium-low heat about 5 minutes, until the bell peppers become limp. Stir in the garlic and cook 5 minutes. Add the tomatoes, bring to a rapid simmer, and cook about 10 minutes, until most of the liquid is reduced. Add salt and pepper to taste. Meanwhile, cook the pasta until al dente in the reheated tomato-blanching water. Drain well and transfer to a warm serving bowl. Top with the pepper-tomato mixture and serve immediately.

Each serving provides:

| | | | |
|---|---|---|---|
| 528 | Calories | 89 g | Carbohydrate |
| 16 g | Protein | 47 mg | Sodium |
| 14 g | Fat | 0 mg | Cholesterol |

# South of the Border Pasta

*A delightful combination of color, texture, and flavors, just like Mexico! Enjoy it hot or at room temperature. This recipe calls for fresh homemade salsa. However, you may substitute commercially prepared fresh salsa, bearing in mind the sodium content will be higher.*

*Yield:* 6 main-course servings

| | | |
|---|---|---|
| Fresh homemade salsa | 2 | cups |
| Stewed tomatoes | 1 | 14.5-ounce can |
| Fresh green beans | 1 | pound |
| Raw pumpkin seeds | ¼ | cup |
| Garlic powder | ¼ | teaspoon |
| Fresh cilantro | 1 | cup, chopped |
| Light sour cream | 1 | cup |
| Feta cheese | 8 | ounces, crumbled |
| Avocado, firmly ripe | 1 | medium |
| Dried pasta | 1 | pound |

**Recommended pasta: penne or other medium tubes**

Prepare fresh salsa (see page 172). Combine the salsa and tomatoes in a large skillet. Bring to a simmer over medium heat. Cook, stirring frequently, until the mixture is reduced to a thick sauce consistency, about 20 minutes. Put several quarts of water on to boil for the pasta. Trim the green beans and cut into 1-inch pieces. Bring a couple of inches of water to a boil in a lidded pot, insert a steaming tray, and steam the beans until just tender. Toast the pumpkin seeds with the garlic powder (see page 20). Cook the pasta until al dente, drain well, and place in a warm bowl. When tomato mixture is reduced add the cilantro and the sour cream. Heat just a moment longer (do not simmer at this stage, as the sour cream will curdle). Pour the sauce over the pasta and toss. Add the feta and toss again. Slice the avocado, arranging the slices in a pretty pattern on top of the pasta. Sprinkle with the toasted pumpkin seeds and serve.

---

### Each serving provides:

| | | | |
|---|---|---|---|
| 574 | Calories | 79 g | Carbohydrate |
| 22 g | Protein | 715 mg | Sodium |
| 21 g | Fat | 47 mg | Cholesterol |

---

# Curried Tomato Sauce with Peanuts and Tempeh

*This may sound like an odd combination, but it is delicious and will meet with favorable reviews at your table.*

*Yield:* 8 main-course servings

| | | |
|---|---|---|
| Tempeh | 8 | ounces |
| Butter | 4 | tablespoons |
| Garlic | 4 | medium cloves, minced |
| Roasted unsalted peanuts | ½ | cup |
| Salt | ½ | teaspoon plus a scant pinch |
| Onion | 1 | medium, coarsely chopped |
| Green bell pepper | 1 | medium, coarsely chopped |
| Curry powder | 2-3 | tablespoons |
| Whole tomatoes | 2 | 28-ounce cans |
| Dry sherry | ½ | cup |
| Fresh parsley, minced | ¼ | cup |
| Dried pasta | 1½ | pounds |

*Recommended pasta:* spaghetti or linguine

With your hands, crumble the tempeh into very small pieces. Melt 2 tablespoons of the butter in a heavy skillet over medium heat. Sauté 1 minced clove of garlic a moment or two, then add the tempeh, peanuts, and a scant pinch of salt. Stir and brown about 10 minutes. Use a spatula to scrape the bottom of the pan from time to time. The fried tempeh that sticks to it will add a delicious crunchiness to the pasta topping. When it is evenly browned, set the tempeh mixture aside.

Melt the remaining 2 tablespoons butter in a high-walled skillet. Add the remaining 3 minced cloves garlic, the onion, bell pepper, and 2 tablespoons curry powder. Stir and sauté 5 minutes. Pour in the tomatoes with their juice and add ½ teaspoon salt. Bring to a simmer over medium heat, taste the sauce, and add more curry powder if you want a spicier sauce. Reduce heat to low and simmer 20–30 minutes, until a nice thick sauce consistency is achieved. Stir in the sherry and heat through. Meanwhile, bring several quarts of water to a boil and cook the pasta until al dente. Drain well. Toss with the tomato sauce in a warm bowl. Coat the top with the tempeh mixture, then sprinkle with the parsley. Serve hot.

| Each serving provides: | | | |
|---|---|---|---|
| 552 | Calories | 83 g | Carbohydrate |
| 21 g | Protein | 547 mg | Sodium |
| 15 g | Fat | 16 mg | Cholesterol |

# Tomato and Lentil Sauce with Feta

*The lentils add protein and stick-to-your-ribs substance to this dish.
It is hearty enough for big appetites.*

*Yield:* 8 main-course servings

| | | |
|---|---|---|
| Dried lentils | 1 | cup |
| Whole tomatoes | 1 | 28-ounce can |
| Onion | 1 | medium, diced |
| Garlic | 3 | medium cloves, minced |
| Dried oregano | 1 | tablespoon |
| Madeira | ¼ | cup |
| Black olives, slivered | 1 | cup |
| Feta cheese | ½ | pound |
| Pepper | | A few grinds |
| Lemon wedges | 1 | per serving |
| Dried pasta | 1 | pound |

*Recommended pasta:* **rigatoni, mostaccioli, or penne**

Carefully sort through the lentils, discarding any tiny rocks you
may find. Rinse the lentils to remove surface dirt, then soak in
a bowl of hot water 2–4 hours. An hour before dinnertime,
pour the tomatoes into a high-walled skillet and add the onion,
garlic, and oregano. Bring to a boil over high heat, then reduce

*The Best 125 Meatless Pasta Dishes*

heat to medium and simmer until somewhat reduced, about 20 minutes. Add the drained lentils and simmer another 20–30 minutes. Lentils should retain a slight firmness. Stir in the Madeira and turn off the heat. Meanwhile, bring several quarts of water to a boil and cook the pasta until al dente. Drain well. Toss in a warm bowl with the lentil sauce, olives, and feta. Grind a little black pepper on top and garnish with lemon wedges.

---

Each serving provides:

| 427 | Calories | 66 g | Carbohydrate |
|------|----------|--------|--------------|
| 19 g | Protein | 633 mg | Sodium |
| 9 g | Fat | 25 mg | Cholesterol |

---

# ✔ Sauce of Tomatoes, Rosemary, and Garbanzos

*This dish makes a wonderful main course, or works well as an accompaniment to grilled fish. The key to this recipe is fresh flat-leaf rosemary. It imparts a less savory, more flowery flavor. The tomatoes can be fresh or canned, depending on the time of year.*

*Yield:* 4 main-course servings

| | | |
|---|---|---|
| **Fresh tomatoes (or 1 28-ounce can whole tomatoes)** | 3 | **pounds** |
| **Garlic** | 2 | **medium cloves, minced** |
| **Fresh flat-leaf rosemary, minced** | 2 | **tablespoons** |
| **Garbanzo beans, cooked** | ½ | **cup** |
| **Asiago cheese, finely grated** | ½ | **cup** |
| **Dried pasta** | 8 | **ounces** |

*Recommended pasta:* **rigatoni or other tubes**

If using canned tomatoes, drain off the juice and save for another use, such as soup. Chop the tomatoes and combine with the garlic and rosemary in a shallow pan. Simmer over high heat to reduce the liquid, about 10 minutes. Bring several quarts of water to a boil and cook the pasta until al dente. If using canned beans, drain and rinse them. Add the beans to the reduced tomato sauce and heat through. Drain the noodles well and transfer to a heated serving bowl. Toss with the sauce and top with the grated cheese. Serve very hot.

---

Each serving provides:

| | | | |
|---|---|---|---|
| 311 | Calories | 55 g | Carbohydrate |
| 14 g | Protein | 137 mg | Sodium |
| 4 g | Fat | 10 mg | Cholesterol |

---

*The Best 125 Meatless Pasta Dishes*

# ✔ Brandied Tomato Sauce

*This sauce has a unique rich flavor without a bit of alcohol bite.*

*Yield:* 4 main-course servings

| | | |
|---|---|---|
| Fresh pear tomatoes | 2 | pounds |
| Olive oil | 2 | tablespoons |
| Garlic | 4 | medium cloves, minced |
| Salt | ½ | teaspoon |
| Pepper | | Several grinds |
| Brandy | ½ | cup |
| Dried pasta | 12 | ounces |

*Recommended pasta:* **spaghetti, fettuccine, or any thin ribbon or strand**

Bring several quarts of water to a boil. Blanch, peel, and seed the tomatoes (see page 21) and chop coarsely. Heat the olive oil in a skillet, add the garlic, and stir a moment or two over medium-high heat. Add the tomatoes, salt, pepper, and brandy, bring to a rapid simmer, and cook 10–12 minutes, until considerably reduced. Meanwhile, cook the pasta until al dente in the reheated tomato-blanching water. Drain well. Toss the hot noodles with the sauce in a warm bowl and serve immediately, garnished with a bit of chopped parsley if you have some on hand.

---

### Each serving provides:

| | | | |
|---|---|---|---|
| 420 | Calories | 74 g | Carbohydrate |
| 13 g | Protein | 296 mg | Sodium |
| 7 g | Fat | 0 mg | Cholesterol |

---

# Green Tomato Sauce with Pasta

*Many an inspired recipe has come to our tables via the garden. This one makes the best of late-harvest green tomatoes.*

*Yield:* 6 main-course servings

| | | |
|---|---|---|
| **Olive oil** | 3 | tablespoons |
| **Green onions** | 3 | thinly sliced |
| **Garlic** | 3 | medium cloves, minced |
| **Fresh green pear tomatoes** | 2 | pounds (12 medium), diced |
| **Japanese eggplant** | 1 | medium, peeled, diced |
| **Dry sherry** | 3 | tablespoons |
| **Dried tomatoes, minced** | ¼ | cup |
| **Water** | ½ | cup |
| **Dried oregano** | 1 | teaspoon |
| **Fresh parsley, minced** | ¼ | cup |
| **Half-and-half** | 2 | tablespoons |
| **Parmesan cheese, finely grated** | ½ | cup |
| **Dried pasta** | 1 | pound |

*Recommended pasta:* **spirals or bowties**

Heat the olive oil in a large skillet and sauté the green onions and garlic about 1 minute. Add the green tomatoes, eggplant, sherry, dried tomatoes, and the water. Cook over medium heat until the green tomatoes are soft, about 20 minutes. Stir often so the tomatoes do not scorch. Meanwhile, bring several quarts of water to a boil and cook the pasta until al dente. Drain well. When the tomatoes are soft, add the oregano and parsley and simmer a few more minutes. Just before serving, stir in the half-and-half. Place the hot pasta on individual warmed plates and top with the sauce. Pass the cheese.

| Each serving provides: | | | |
|---|---|---|---|
| 445 | Calories | 70 g | Carbohydrate |
| 16 g | Protein | 186 mg | Sodium |
| 11 g | Fat | 8 mg | Cholesterol |

# Dairy-Based Stovetop Sauces

Calorie and cholesterol concerns aside, who doesn't love pasta with cream and cheese? For the sake of optimum health, these rather rich dishes shouldn't appear on your table daily. But unless you're on a restricted diet, and on days when your fat intake from other sources has been minimal, you can splurge on a dairy-rich concoction without a twinge of guilt.

In fact, many of the recipes in this section aren't overly fatty. Although they do all contain some quantity of dairy products, we consistently use lower-fat versions of sour cream, cottage cheese, ricotta cheese, yogurt, and milk. (Do not, however, mistake "imitation" sour cream for a reduced-fat type, as you will be disappointed with the synthetic flavor and consistency.)

If you can't locate these lowfat alternatives in your supermarket, ask your grocer to order them. Or you may prefer the unabashed richness of whole-milk products. Use them, if you wish, with equal success in our recipes.

The most basic cream sauce starts with a roux made by melting butter and stirring in an equivalent amount of flour. This thick paste is stirred and browned just a bit before whisking in warmed milk or cream. The mixture is gently simmered, whisking frequently, until it is thickened and smooth. (The basic proportions are 1 tablespoon each butter and flour to 1 cup milk.) Spices can be heated in the butter before other ingredients are added, or season the finished sauce to your liking. A little salt and pepper are almost always used; from there you are limited only by your imagination.

The assortment of recipes we offer here will introduce you to other simple techniques for dairy-based sauces. Once you learn the basics, be brave and playful and see what new worlds of flavor you can discover.

# Leeks, Carrot, and Pecans with Nutmeg Cream

*The subtle flavors of pecans and nutmeg bring this beautiful light dish together.*

*Yield:* 6 side-dish servings

| | | |
|---|---|---|
| Leeks | 2 | medium (about ¾ pound) |
| Carrot | 1 | medium |
| Butter | 3 | tablespoons |
| Flour | 1 | tablespoon |
| Salt | ½ | teaspoon |
| Freshly grated nutmeg | 1 | teaspoon |
| Half-and-half | 1 | cup |
| White wine | ¾ | cup |
| Raw pecans, minced | ½ | cup |
| Dried pasta | 8 | ounces |

*Recommended pasta:* spinach angel hair or any thin strand

Trim the root end and most of the green portion from the leeks and discard. Cut leeks in half lengthwise and rinse under cold water to remove any grit lodged between their concentric layers. Blot dry. Cut crosswise at a slant into thin half rounds. Cut the carrot into thin 1-inch matchsticks. Put several quarts of water on to boil for the pasta. Melt the butter in a large skillet, add the leeks and carrot, and sauté over medium-high heat, stirring often, 10 minutes. The vegetables will begin to brown and become limp. Sprinkle with the flour, salt, and nutmeg and stir to distribute evenly. Add the half-and-half. Reduce heat to low, stir, and simmer 5 minutes. Add the wine and simmer another 5 minutes. The sauce will reduce a bit but will still be a thin consistency. Meanwhile, roast the minced pecans (see page 20). Cook the pasta until al dente and drain well. Just before serving, stir the pecans into the cream sauce, reserving a few for garnish. Gently toss the hot noodles with the sauce and garnish with reserved pecans.

---

Each serving provides:

| | | | |
|---|---|---|---|
| 334 | Calories | 38 g | Carbohydrate |
| 8 g | Protein | 262 mg | Sodium |
| 15 g | Fat | 25 mg | Cholesterol |

---

# ✔ Pasta Carbonara Senza Carne

*In classic carbonara style, raw egg is the basis for this rich and flavorful pasta topping. It comes together quickly and will please even the pickiest gourmand.*

*Yield:* 8 side-dish servings

| | | |
|---|---|---|
| Onions | 2 | medium |
| Butter | 4 | tablespoons |
| Half-and-half | ½ | cup |
| Egg yolks | 3 | |
| Pine nuts | ½ | cup |
| Fresh basil leaves, chopped | 1 | cup, loosely packed |
| Freshly grated nutmeg | ¼ | teaspoon |
| Romano cheese, finely grated | ½ | cup |
| Dried pasta | 1 | pound |

*Recommended pasta:* **vermicelli, spaghettini, or any thin strand**

Halve the onions lengthwise, then thinly slice the halves. Melt the butter in a large skillet and sauté the onions over very low heat 20 minutes, until very tender. Bring several quarts of water to a boil and cook the pasta until al dente. Meanwhile, in a small saucepan, heat the half-and-half until barely warm. Toast the pine nuts (see page 20). Just before the pasta is done, beat the egg yolks lightly in a large, barely warm serving bowl. Slowly whisk the warm cream into the egg yolks (if cream is too hot it will scramble the eggs, so let it cool a bit if necessary before proceeding). Stir in the onions. Quickly but thoroughly drain the cooked pasta. Add the very hot pasta to the egg mixture and toss until pasta is well coated.* Add the basil, nutmeg, cheese, and pine nuts and toss again. Serve immediately on warmed plates.

---

Each serving provides:

| 224 | Calories | 6 g | Carbohydrate |
|---|---|---|---|
| 8 g | Protein | 171 mg | Sodium |
| 21 g | Fat | 141 mg | Cholesterol |

---

*Due to the controversy concerning raw eggs and salmonella bacteria, add eggs when pasta is very hot, *not* warm. For further information, contact your local office of the U.S. Department of Agriculture.

# ✔ Oyster Mushrooms with Cilantro and Cream

*This recipe was inspired by the desire for a light meal following a week of holiday feasting! Look for fresh oyster mushrooms at a well-stocked gourmet or natural food store.*

*Yield:* 4 side-dish servings

| Butter | 2 | tablespoons |
|---|---|---|
| Fresh oyster mushrooms | 4 | ounces, coarsely chopped |
| Fresh cilantro, minced | 2 | tablespoons |
| White wine | 3 | tablespoons |
| Dried tomatoes, minced | 1 | tablespoon |
| Light sour cream | ½ | cup |
| Half-and-half | ¼ | cup |
| Dried pasta | 8 | ounces |

*Recommended pasta:* penne or other small tubes

Melt the butter in a small skillet and sauté the mushrooms until they release their juice and become limp. Bring several quarts of water to a boil and cook the pasta until al dente. Drain well. Meanwhile, stir the cilantro, wine, dried tomatoes, sour cream, and half-and-half into the mushrooms. Warm thoroughly over very low heat. Toss the pasta in a warm serving bowl with the mushroom mixture. Serve immediately.

---

Each serving provides:

| 339 | Calories | 49 g | Carbohydrate |
|---|---|---|---|
| 11 g | Protein | 112 mg | Sodium |
| 10 g | Fat | 21 mg | Cholesterol |

---

# ✔ Light Garlic Cream Sauce

*This is quick to make and really delicious. Serve it as a side dish with grilled fish or tofu, if you wish.*

*Yield:* 4 side-dish servings

| | |
|---|---|
| **Butter** | 2   tablespoons |
| **Garlic** | 3   medium cloves, minced |
| **Lowfat milk** | ½ cup |
| **Half-and-half** | ½ cup |
| **Freshly grated nutmeg** | ⅛ teaspoon |
| **Parmesan cheese, finely grated** | ½ cup |
| **Peas, fresh or frozen** | ½ cup |
| **Dried pasta** | 8   ounces |

*Recommended pasta:* **fettuccine or spirals**

Put several quarts of water on to boil for the pasta. Melt the butter in a small skillet over low heat. Add the garlic and sauté, stirring often, until just beginning to brown. Whisk in the milk and half-and-half. Add the nutmeg (freshly grated makes all the difference). Cook over medium-high heat about 10 minutes, whisking often. Meanwhile, cook the noodles until al dente. While they are cooking, whisk the Parmesan into the sauce. Stir in the peas and heat through. Toss the cooked noodles in a warm serving bowl with the sauce. Serve immediately.

---

Each serving provides:

| | | | |
|---|---|---|---|
| 388 | Calories | 49 g | Carbohydrate |
| 15 g | Protein | 319 mg | Sodium |
| 14 g | Fat | 37 mg | Cholesterol |

---

# Asparagus and Mushrooms
# in Tarragon Cream

*A local Italian restaurant serves a version of this dish during
asparagus season. We created our own, lighter version, with the
addition of tarragon. It's a perennial hit.*

*Yield:* 6 main-course servings

| | | |
|---|---|---|
| Asparagus | 2 | pounds |
| Butter | 2 | tablespoons |
| Garlic | 3 | medium cloves, minced |
| Dried tarragon | 1 | tablespoon |
| Mushrooms | ¾ | pound, thickly sliced |
| Salt | ½ | teaspoon |
| Flour | 1 | tablespoon |
| Half-and-half | 1½ | cups |
| Freshly grated nutmeg | ½ | teaspoon |
| Parmesan cheese, finely grated | ½ | cup |
| Pepper | | To taste |
| Lemon wedges | 1 | per serving |
| Dried pasta | 12 | ounces |

*Recommended pasta:* fettuccine or linguine

Break off the tough stem ends of the asparagus stalks, and cut
the asparagus at a slant into 3-inch lengths. Melt the butter in a
large skillet, add the garlic and tarragon, and stir to distribute.
Add the asparagus and mushrooms, sprinkle with the salt, and
stir and sauté over medium heat about 10 minutes. Sprinkle
the flour over the vegetables and stir to distribute. Add the
half-and-half and nutmeg; reduce heat to low. Bring to a sim-

*The Best 125 Meatless Pasta Dishes*

mer and cook about 5 minutes, until the sauce is slightly thickened. Meanwhile, bring several quarts of water to a boil and cook the pasta until al dente. Toss the well-drained pasta with the sauce in a warm serving bowl. Add the Parmesan and a few grinds of pepper and toss again. Serve immediately, passing additional Parmesan, if desired, and the lemon wedges.

---

Each serving provides:

| | | | |
|---|---|---|---|
| 402 | Calories | 53 g | Carbohydrate |
| 16 g | Protein | 406 mg | Sodium |
| 15 g | Fat | 39 mg | Cholesterol |

---

# ✔ Creamy Pasta with Artichokes and Dried Tomatoes

*You will enjoy this delicate blending of flavors.*

*Yield:* 4 main-course servings

| | | |
|---|---|---|
| Pine nuts | 2 | tablespoons |
| Olive oil | 3 | tablespoons |
| Garlic | 2 | medium cloves, minced |
| Flour | 2 | tablespoons |
| Lowfat milk | 1 | cup |
| Dried tomatoes, chopped | ¼ | cup |
| White wine | ¼ | cup |
| Dried tarragon | 1 | teaspoon |
| Marinated artichoke hearts | 1 | 6-ounce jar |
| Balsamic vinegar | 1 | teaspoon |
| Dried pasta | 8 | ounces |

*Recommended pasta:* **egg noodles or fettuccine**

Put several quarts of water on to boil for the pasta. Toast the pine nuts (see page 20). Heat the olive oil over very low heat in a cast-iron skillet; add the garlic and cook several seconds. Stir in the flour, cooking it about 1 minute to heat through, but not browning. Whisk in the milk, a bit at a time. Continue to cook, whisking often, until mixture is slightly thickened, about 8–10 minutes. Add the dried tomatoes, wine, and tarragon. Stir often while cooking over low heat about 3 more minutes. Meanwhile, cook the noodles until al dente. Drain well. Just before serving, drain and chop the artichoke hearts, stir them into the sauce, and heat through. Toss the pasta with the sauce in a warm bowl. Add the pine nuts and vinegar, tossing to distribute evenly.

| Each serving provides: | | | |
|---|---|---|---|
| 430 | Calories | 55 g | Carbohydrate |
| 13 g | Protein | 96 mg | Sodium |
| 18 g | Fat | 56 mg | Cholesterol |

# ✔ Basic Alfredo Sauce

*Alfredo is the quintessential rich and creamy pasta sauce. Here we present a very basic recipe. It is simply wonderful on its own, or you can top the pasta with steamed vegetables or sautéed mushrooms to create a substantial main course.*

*Yield:* 6 side-dish servings

| | | |
|---|---|---|
| **Half-and-half** | 2 | **cups** |
| **Butter** | 2 | **tablespoons** |
| **Garlic** | 3 | **medium cloves, minced** |
| **Freshly grated nutmeg** | ½ | **teaspoon** |
| **Salt** | ¼ | **teaspoon** |
| **Pepper** | | **To taste** |
| **Egg** | 1 | **large, lightly beaten** |
| **Parmesan cheese, finely grated** | 1 | **cup** |
| **Dried pasta** | 12 | **ounces** |

*Recommended pasta:* **fettuccine or linguine**

Bring several quarts of water to a boil and cook the pasta until al dente. Drain briefly. Meanwhile, warm the half-and-half in a small saucepan over very low heat. Melt the butter in a high-walled skillet and sauté the garlic over low heat about 3 minutes. Add the warm cream, the nutmeg, salt, and pepper. Continue to cook over low heat until the sauce reaches a simmer. As soon as it begins to bubble, add the pasta and remove from the heat. Push the noodles to the sides of the pan to make a well in the center. Pour the beaten egg into this well and, quickly but carefully, begin to lift and toss the pasta with the sauce until the egg is smoothly incorporated.* Add the Parmesan and continue lifting and tossing until it is smoothly incorporated and everything is well combined. Serve immediately on warm plates, passing more grated cheese and the pepper grinder, if desired. If the pasta seems more gooey than creamy, drizzle on a bit of hot water and toss again, until the right consistency is achieved.

---

Each serving provides:

| 438 | Calories | 47 g | Carbohydrate |
|---|---|---|---|
| 18 g | Protein | 480 mg | Sodium |
| 20 g | Fat | 88 mg | Cholesterol |

---

*Due to the controversy concerning raw eggs and salmonella bacteria, add eggs when the sauce is very hot, *not* warm. For further information, contact your local office of the U.S. Department of Agriculture.

# Broccoli, Dried Tomato, and Ginger Cream

*This unusual combination of flavors will surprise and delight your guests. Serve it on an unusual Asian noodle, like buckwheat soba, to complete the effect.*

*Yield:* 6 main-course servings

| | | |
|---|---|---|
| Sesame seeds | 1 | tablespoon |
| Olive oil | 2 | tablespoons |
| Garlic | 2 | medium cloves, minced |
| Mushrooms | ½ | pound, sliced |
| Onion | 1 | medium, chopped |
| Dried tomatoes, slivered | ⅓ | cup |
| Salt | ¼ | teaspoon |
| Dry sherry | 2 | tablespoons |
| Light sour cream | 2 | cups |
| Lowfat milk | ⅓ | cup |
| Fresh ginger, grated | 1 | tablespoon |
| Soy sauce | 1 | tablespoon |
| Broccoli, chopped | 3 | cups, loosely packed |
| Cayenne pepper | | To taste |
| Dried pasta | 12 | ounces |

**Recommended pasta:** soba, udon, or any thin strand

Put several quarts of water on to boil for the pasta. Toast the sesame seeds (see page 20). In a large skillet, heat the olive oil and stir in the garlic, mushrooms, onion, and dried tomatoes. Add the salt, stir, and sauté 8 minutes. Turn off the heat and stir in the sherry. In a large bowl, whisk together the sour cream, milk, ginger, and soy sauce, then stir in the sautéed vegetables. Heat gently in a double boiler or place the bowl over the boiling pasta pot. Keep warm. Cook the pasta until al dente, adding broccoli the last 4 minutes of cooking time. Drain well. Toss with the sauce in a warm serving bowl. Sprinkle with the sesame seeds and cayenne, if you enjoy a spicy flavor. Serve on warmed plates.

| Each serving provides: | | | |
|---|---|---|---|
| 423 | Calories | 64 g | Carbohydrate |
| 16 g | Protein | 399 mg | Sodium |
| 12 g | Fat | 1 mg | Cholesterol |

# Curried Creamed Eggs

*When you're in the mood for comfort food, this rich and creamy curry sauce will fit the bill.*

*Yield:* 8 main-course servings

| | | |
|---|---|---|
| Peas, fresh or frozen | ¾ | cup |
| Eggs | 4 | large |
| Lowfat milk | 1½ | cups |
| Butter | 3 | tablespoons |
| Onion | 1 | medium, coarsely chopped |
| Curry powder | 1 | tablespoon |
| Flour | 3 | tablespoons |
| Salt | ½ | teaspoon |
| Carrot | 1 | medium, thinly sliced |
| Dried pasta | 1 | pound |

*Recommended pasta:* spinach ribbons or whole wheat spirals

If using frozen peas, set them out to thaw at room temperature. Hardboil the eggs and cool in very cold water to make the peeling easier. When eggs have cooled, peel them and crumble the yolks into a bowl. Chop the whites coarsely and set aside with the yolks. Warm the milk in a saucepan over very low heat to the scalding point (do not simmer). Put a large pot of water on to boil for the pasta. Melt the butter in a skillet over medium heat. Sauté the onion until it is limp, about 5 minutes. Add curry and flour and stir over very low heat 3 minutes longer. Continue to stir or whisk as you pour in the warm milk. Add the salt. Increase heat to medium. Stir and cook the sauce until it thickens enough to thinly coat a spoon, about 5 minutes. Add the peas and stir a minute longer. Add the eggs and stir gently to distribute them evenly throughout the sauce. Meanwhile, cook the pasta until al dente. Drop the carrot slices into the pasta pot just a minute before the pasta is al dente. Drain well. Arrange cooked pasta with carrots on a platter and pour the sauce over them. Serve very hot.

---

Each serving provides:

| | | | |
|---|---|---|---|
| 337 | Calories | 51 g | Carbohydrate |
| 14 g | Protein | 260 mg | Sodium |
| 8 g | Fat | 120 mg | Cholesterol |

---

# Mushrooms Stroganoff

*A recipe we have both been making for years, this mushroom stroganoff is delicious and hearty enough to replace the beef version without any sense of sacrifice.*

*Yield:* 4 main-course servings

| | | |
|---|---|---|
| Butter | 4 | tablespoons |
| Garlic | 2 | medium cloves, minced |
| Mushrooms | 1½ | pounds, thinly sliced |
| Onion | 1 | small, coarsely chopped |
| Water | 1 | cup |
| Vegetable broth cube | 1 | |
| Flour | 2 | tablespoons |
| Tomato paste | 1 | tablespoon |
| Light sour cream | ½ | cup |
| White wine | 2 | tablespoons |
| Dried pasta | 12 | ounces |

*Recommended pasta:* **fettuccine or linguine**

Melt 2 tablespoons of the butter in a high-walled skillet, stir in the garlic, then add the mushrooms and onion and stir again. Sauté over low heat until the onion is golden and the mushrooms are limp and have released their juices, about 15 minutes. Meanwhile, heat the water and broth cube in a small saucepan and keep warm. Bring several quarts of water to a boil and cook the pasta until al dente. Drain well. Meanwhile, in a separate skillet, melt the remaining 2 tablespoons butter over medium heat. Add the flour and stir 1 minute, until it begins to brown. Whisk in the vegetable broth, then the tomato paste. Cook over medium heat, whisking frequently, until sauce is smooth and thickened, about 5 minutes. Turn off heat and stir in the sour cream. Fold in the mushroom mixture and wine. Combine well. Toss with the hot noodles in a warm bowl and serve immediately.

Each serving provides:

| 330 | Calories | 51 g | Carbohydrate |
| 10 g | Protein | 126 mg | Sodium |
| 9 g | Fat | 21 mg | Cholesterol |

# ✔ Ricotta with Nutmeg and Peas

*This dish comes together very quickly, making it a perfect choice
when friends drop by and you're in the mood for a light and delicious
meal. Serve it with garlic bread and a tart, leafy salad.*

*Yield:* 4 main-course servings

| | | |
|---|---|---|
| **Part-skim ricotta cheese** | **15** | **ounces** |
| **Butter** | **4** | **tablespoons** |
| **Peas, fresh or frozen** | **1½** | **cups** |
| **Freshly grated nutmeg** | **½** | **teaspoon** |
| **Salt** | **¼** | **teaspoon** |
| **Pepper** | | **A few grinds** |
| **Parmesan cheese, finely grated** | **½** | **cup** |
| **Dried pasta** | **12** | **ounces** |

*Recommended pasta:* **small tubes or spirals**

Bring the ricotta and butter to room temperature. Since the
sauce will not be heated, you do not want your ingredients to
be cold. Bring several quarts of water to a boil and cook the
pasta until al dente, adding the peas for the final 2 minutes of
cooking time. Meanwhile, mash the ricotta and butter in a bowl

*The Best 125 Meatless Pasta Dishes*

with the nutmeg, salt, and pepper. Set the bowl in a warm spot on the stove while you wait for the pasta to cook. Drain the pasta and peas briefly, allowing a bit of water to remain on the noodles. Toss with the ricotta mixture and the Parmesan in a warm bowl. Serve immediately on warmed plates, sprinkled with additional Parmesan and a little nutmeg.

Each serving provides:

| 669 | Calories | 78 g | Carbohydrate |
|-----|----------|------|--------------|
| 31 g | Protein | 621 mg | Sodium |
| 25 g | Fat | 79 mg | Cholesterol |

# ✔ Savory Ricotta Sauce

*This dish is wonderful any time of the year, but especially good on a cold winter night. It has a rich, savory flavor that you will enjoy.*

*Yield:* 8 side-dish servings

| | | |
|---|---|---|
| Olive oil | ¼ | cup |
| Onion | 1 | medium, diced |
| Soy sauce | ½ | teaspoon |
| Worcestershire sauce | ½ | teaspoon |
| Part-skim ricotta cheese | 1 | pound |
| Fresh parsley, minced | ¼ | cup |
| Fresh basil leaves, chopped | ¼ | cup |
| Green onions | 2, | minced |
| Parmesan cheese, finely grated | ⅓ | cup |
| Salt and pepper | | To taste |
| Dried pasta | 1 | pound |

*Recommended pasta:* penne, rigatoni, or other tube

*The Best 125 Meatless Pasta Dishes*

Put several quarts of water on to boil for the pasta. Heat the olive oil in a large skillet. Add the onion and sauté over very low heat until translucent, about 5 minutes. Stir in the soy sauce and Worcestershire sauce, remove from the heat, and set aside. In a saucepan, mix together the ricotta, parsley, basil, green onion, and Parmesan. Stir in the cooked onion. Meanwhile, cook the pasta until al dente. Drain, reserving ½ cup of the cooking water, and transfer to a warm serving bowl. Add the cooking water to the ricotta mixture and warm gently over low heat. Toss the sauce with the hot noodles and serve immediately.

---

Each serving provides:

| 374 | Calories | 47 g | Carbohydrate |
|------|----------|--------|--------------|
| 16 g | Protein | 176 mg | Sodium |
| 14 g | Fat | 21 mg | Cholesterol |

---

# Creamy Red Bell Pepper Sauce with Tarragon

*The rather dry texture of ricotta cheese is balanced in this dish by the juicy tang of roasted red bell peppers. Instead of roasting your own, you could buy commercially prepared roasted red bell peppers at a good gourmet supermarket. For this recipe use a cup, drained and chopped.*

*Yield:* 4 side-dish servings

| | | |
|---|---|---|
| Red bell peppers | 2 | medium |
| Butter | 2 | tablespoons |
| Garlic | 1 | medium clove, minced |
| Dried tarragon | 2 | teaspoons |
| Salt | ½ | teaspoon |
| Pepper | | A few grinds |
| Part-skim ricotta cheese | 1 | cup |
| Plain lowfat yogurt | ½ | cup |
| Olive oil | 2 | tablespoons |
| Parmesan cheese, finely grated | ⅓ | cup |
| Green onions | 5 | minced |
| Dried pasta | 10 | ounces |

*Recommended pasta:* vermicelli or linguine

Roast, peel, and seed the bell peppers (see page 21) and chop coarsely. Put several quarts of water on to boil. Melt the butter in a heavy skillet and sauté the peppers, garlic, tarragon, ¼ teaspoon of the salt, and a few grinds of pepper 10 minutes.

Meanwhile, whisk the ricotta and yogurt with the remaining ¼ teaspoon salt. Cook the pasta until al dente. Add the ricotta mixture to the peppers and stir over low heat until sauce is beginning to simmer, about 5 minutes. Toss hot pasta in a warm bowl with the olive oil and Parmesan, then with the sauce and green onions. Serve immediately.

| Each serving provides: | | | |
|---|---|---|---|
| 531 | Calories | 62 g | Carbohydrate |
| 22 g | Protein | 586 mg | Sodium |
| 22 g | Fat | 43 mg | Cholesterol |

# ✔ Mushrooms Paprikash

*If you can get fresh dill, use it for this recipe. It imparts a wonderfully alive flavor! And be sure to reserve a few sprigs for garnish.*

*Yield:* 6 main-dish servings

| Ingredient | Amount | |
|---|---|---|
| Butter | 2 | tablespoons |
| Garlic | 2 | medium cloves, minced |
| Paprika | 1½ | tablespoons |
| Mushrooms | 1 | pound, thinly sliced |
| Salt | ¼ | teaspoon |
| Light sour cream | 2 | cups |
| Prepared horseradish | 2 | tablespoons |
| Dill | 1 | tablespoon dried or 2 tablespoons fresh |
| Cheddar cheese | 4 | ounces, grated |
| Dried pasta | 12 | ounces |

*Recommended pasta:* fettuccine or linguine

Put several quarts of water on to boil. Melt the butter in a skillet, stir in the garlic and paprika, then add the mushrooms and stir to coat with butter and seasonings. Add the salt and sauté over low heat until the mushrooms release their liquid and it is somewhat reduced, about 7 minutes—only a few tablespoons of the liquid should remain. In a bowl, combine the sour cream, horseradish, and dill. Add this mixture to the cooked mushrooms and stir to combine well. Heat gently about 5 minutes, until sauce is hot (be careful not to heat too rapidly, as the sour cream may curdle). Meanwhile, cook the pasta until al dente and drain well. Toss with the sauce and cheese in a warm bowl, turning gently to distribute evenly. Serve with a sprinkling of dill (or a garnish of fresh dill sprigs) and paprika.

Each serving provides:

| 349 | Calories | 48 g | Carbohydrate |
|---|---|---|---|
| 14 g | Protein | 260 mg | Sodium |
| 11 g | Fat | 30 mg | Cholesterol |

# ✔ Green Chili Sauce with Sour Cream

*Canned mild green chilies are the main ingredient in this rich and piquant sauce. It's the kind of sauce that might be served in Mexico if pasta were a staple there.*

*Yield:* 6 side-dish servings

| | | |
|---|---|---|
| Raw sunflower seeds | 3 | tablespoons |
| Olive oil | 2 | tablespoons |
| Onion | 1 | medium, coarsely chopped |
| Garlic | 2 | medium cloves, minced |
| Dried oregano | 1 | tablespoon |
| Canned whole green chilies | 1 | cup, loosely packed |
| Salt | ¼ | teaspoon |
| Black pepper | | A few grinds |
| Red bell pepper | 1 | medium, grated |
| Light sour cream | 1 | cup |
| Fresh cilantro, minced | ¼ | cup |
| Jack cheese, grated | ½ | cup |
| Dried pasta | 1 | pound |

*Recommended pasta:* vermicelli or fettuccine

Put several quarts of water on to boil. Toast the sunflower seeds (see page 20) and set aside. In a heavy skillet, heat the olive oil and sauté the onion and garlic with the oregano 7–10 minutes, until onion is limp and transparent. Place the sautéed onions and garlic, the sunflower seeds, chilies, salt, and black pepper in a food processor or blender jar. Puree until thick and homogenous. Transfer to a saucepan, stir in the grated bell pepper, and bring to the steaming stage over low heat. Combine the sour cream with several tablespoons of the hot chili mixture in a bowl. Stir until smooth. Stir in the cilantro. Add the sour cream mixture to the chili sauce, stir to incorporate, and remove from the heat. Meanwhile, cook the pasta until al dente and drain well. Toss with the sauce and cheese and serve with a sprinkling of cilantro or oregano.

Each serving provides:

| 452 | Calories | 67 g | Carbohydrate |
| 16 g | Protein | 339 mg | Sodium |
| 14 g | Fat | 8 mg | Cholesterol |

# Spicy Cannellini and Green Beans with Raisins

*This unusual blending of ingredients is delicious and protein-packed. It makes a particularly satisfying meal after an active day.*

*Yield:* 4 main-course servings

| | | |
|---|---|---|
| Dried cannellini or navy beans | ½ | cup |
| Fresh green beans | ½ | pound |
| Red onion | 1 | small |
| Olive oil | 2 | tablespoons |
| Garlic | 2 | medium cloves, minced |
| Dry sherry | 2 | tablespoons |
| Golden raisins | ½ | cup |
| Lowfat milk | ½ | cup |
| Plain lowfat yogurt | ⅔ | cup |
| Light sour cream | ½ | cup |
| Curry powder | 1-2 | tablespoons |
| Dried tomatoes, diced | ¼ | cup |
| Raw walnuts, chopped | ¼ | cup |
| Dried red chili flakes | ⅛ | teaspoon |
| Dried pasta | 8 | ounces |

*Recommended pasta:* **penne or other tubes**

Sort and rinse the cannellini beans and soak several hours or overnight. Drain, cover with fresh water in a large pot, and bring to a simmer. Cook uncovered 25 minutes, until just tender. Drain, reserving the liquid for a soup stock or other use. Put several quarts of water on to boil for the pasta. Trim the green beans and cut at a slant into 1-inch pieces. Cut the onion in half lengthwise and thickly slice each half. Heat the olive oil

*The Best 125 Meatless Pasta Dishes*

in a large skillet and sauté the onion and garlic several minutes, until onion is limp and transparent. Stir in the cooked cannellini beans, the green beans, sherry, and raisins. Stir and sauté 2 minutes longer. In a bowl, stir together the milk, yogurt, sour cream, curry powder, and dried tomato. Add to the skillet, cover, and cook over low heat about 10 minutes, until green beans are tender-crisp. Toast the walnuts with the chili flakes (see page 20). Meanwhile, cook the pasta until al dente and drain well. Toss the pasta with the sauce in a warm bowl. Top with the walnuts and serve immediately.

---

Each serving provides:

| | | | |
|---|---|---|---|
| 585 | Calories | 91 g | Carbohydrate |
| 22 g | Protein | 107 mg | Sodium |
| 16 g | Fat | 3 mg | Cholesterol |

---

# Brandied Mushrooms
# with Two Cheeses

*Porcini, Italian field mushrooms, are one of nature's richest-tasting foods. They are too expensive for most of us to enjoy in large quantities; fortunately, a little goes a long way.*

*Yield:* 6 main-course servings

| | |
|---|---|
| Dried porcini | ½ ounce |
| Fontina cheese | 4 ounces |
| Butter | 4 tablespoons |
| Mushrooms | ½ pound, thinly sliced |
| Flour | 2 tablespoons |
| Lowfat milk | 1 cup |
| Brandy | ¼ cup |
| Salt | ½ teaspoon |
| Parmesan cheese, finely grated | ½ cup |
| Fresh parsley, minced | ¼ cup |
| Freshly grated nutmeg | 1 teaspoon |
| Dried pasta | 12 ounces |

*Recommended pasta:* fettuccine, linguine, or any thin ribbon or strand

Soak the porcini in 1 cup warm water about half an hour. Lift the porcini from the water and chop coarsely. Strain the soaking liquid through a paper coffee filter and set aside. Dice the fontina into ¼-inch pieces. Put several quarts of water on to boil for the pasta. Melt the butter and sauté the porcini over medium heat 5 minutes, then add the sliced mushrooms and sauté 10 minutes longer, until they have released their liquid and are limp. Sprinkle on the flour and stir to distribute. Stir in the milk, brandy, and ½ cup of the porcini soaking liquid. Add the salt and simmer the mixture over low heat 5–10 minutes, until slightly thickened. Meanwhile, cook the pasta until al dente and drain well. In a warm bowl, combine the mushroom sauce, the fontina and Parmesan, and the pasta. Gently stir and turn the noodles until the cheese is melted and the sauce is evenly distributed. Garnish with the parsley and nutmeg and serve immediately.

---

Each serving provides:

| 248 | Calories | 8 g | Carbohydrate |
| 11 g | Protein | 587 mg | Sodium |
| 17 g | Fat | 51 mg | Cholesterol |

---

# ✔ Sauce of Feta, Fresh Herbs, and Cashews

*For this recipe, it is preferable to put the garlic through a press rather than mincing it with a knife, as you want the garlic to liquefy a bit and distribute well in the oil. If you're using dill or oregano, 2 tablespoons will not be too much. With the woodier rosemary, use only 1 tablespoon.*

*Yield:* 6 side-dish servings

| | | |
|---|---|---|
| Olive oil | ⅓ | cup |
| Garlic | 2 | medium cloves, pressed |
| Fresh oregano, dill, or rosemary, minced | 1-2 | tablespoons |
| Parmesan cheese, finely grated | ⅓ | cup |
| Feta cheese, crumbled | 1 | cup |
| Roasted unsalted cashews | 1 | cup |
| Lemon wedges | 1 | per serving |
| Dried pasta | 12 | ounces |

*Recommended pasta:* spirals or vermicelli

A few hours before mealtime, stir together the olive oil, garlic, and minced herbs in a small saucepan. Set aside at room temperature so the flavors can blend. When ready to eat, bring several quarts of water to a boil and cook the pasta until al dente. Drain well. Meanwhile, barely heat the olive oil mixture over low heat. In a warm bowl, toss the hot noodles with the oil and Parmesan, then with the feta and cashews. Serve immediately with a lemon wedge on each plate. Pass the pepper grinder, if desired.

Each serving provides:

| 528 | Calories | 51 g | Carbohydrate |
|---|---|---|---|
| 16 g | Protein | 359 mg | Sodium |
| 30 g | Fat | 24 mg | Cholesterol |

*Dairy-Based Stovetop Sauces*

# Creamy Eggplant and Gorgonzola Sauce

*In this dish, the eggplant is cooked long enough to become a sauce in itself. It blends beautifully with the piquant gorgonzola.*

*Yield:* 8 side-dish servings

| | | |
|---|---|---|
| **Eggplant** | 2 | small (about 1½ pounds) |
| **Chard** | 1 | bunch (about ¾ pound) |
| **Onion** | 1 | medium |
| **Water** | ½ | cup |
| **Raw walnuts, chopped** | 1 | cup |
| **Salt** | ¼ | teaspoon |
| **Fresh basil leaves** | 1 | cup, loosely packed |
| **Olive oil** | 2 | tablespoons |
| **Gorgonzola cheese, crumbled** | 1 | cup |
| **Dried pasta** | 1 | pound |

*Recommended pasta:* **penne or rigatoni**

Choose small, firm eggplants. Without peeling, dice them. Wash chard, remove and sliver the stems, and tear the leaves into pieces. Cut the onion lengthwise in half, then thinly slice each half. Toast the walnuts (see page 20). In a high-walled skillet, heat the water to boiling. Place the eggplant, chard stems, and onion in the water, sprinkle with the salt, and simmer, covered, over low heat 20 minutes. Vegetables will be very soft. Stir in the chard leaves and basil and simmer, uncovered, about 5 minutes, or until liquid is almost gone. Meanwhile, bring several quarts of water to a boil and cook the pasta until al dente. Drain well. Toss with the olive oil, then with the eggplant mixture, then with the cheese and half the walnuts. Serve in a large, shallow bowl garnished with a few basil leaves and the remaining walnuts. Pass the pepper grinder, if desired.

---

Each serving provides:

| | | | |
|---|---|---|---|
| 431 | Calories | 53 g | Carbohydrate |
| 15 g | Protein | 396 mg | Sodium |
| 19 g | Fat | 13 mg | Cholesterol |

---

# Blue Cheese Pasta and Veggies

*The combination of garlic and blue cheese is intensely rich and aromatic and not for the faint of heart. The simplicity of preparation is an added bonus.*

*Yield:* 8 main-course servings

| | | |
|---|---|---|
| **Broccoli, chopped** | 3 | **cups, loosely packed** |
| **Carrots** | 2 | **medium, thinly sliced** |
| **Crookneck squash or zucchini** | 2 | **medium, diced** |
| **Olive oil** | ⅓ | **cup** |
| **Butter** | 3 | **tablespoons** |
| **Garlic** | 2 | **medium cloves, minced** |
| **Cayenne pepper** | ¼ | **teaspoon** |
| **Blue cheese** | 8 | **ounces, crumbled** |
| **Parmesan cheese, finely grated** | ½ | **cup** |
| **Dried pasta** | 1 | **pound** |

*Recommended pasta:* **linguine, tagliarini, or spaghetti**

Put several quarts of water on to boil for the pasta. Use plenty of water, as it must accommodate the vegetables as well. Cook the pasta until al dente, adding the broccoli, carrots, and squash for the last 3 minutes of cooking time. Meanwhile, warm the olive oil, butter, garlic, and cayenne in a small skillet or saucepan over low heat for about 5 minutes. See that the oil heats slowly so the garlic doesn't burn, though it may brown a little. When the pasta and vegetables are al dente, drain thoroughly and drizzle the oil mixture evenly over them in a warm bowl. Toss to distribute, then toss again with the blue cheese and Parmesan. Serve very hot.

Each serving provides:

| | | | |
|---|---|---|---|
| 482 | Calories | 49 g | Carbohydrate |
| 18 g | Protein | 573 mg | Sodium |
| 24 g | Fat | 38 mg | Cholesterol |

# Paprika Blue Cheese Sauce with Green Beans and Pecans

*Just enough blue cheese is used to impart a sharp tang and intriguing aroma. The smoky crunch of the toasted pecans completes the picture perfectly. This is a great way to enjoy tiny new green beans from the garden.*

*Yield:* 8 main-course servings

| | | |
|---|---|---|
| Slender green beans | 1 | pound |
| Butter | 2 | tablespoons |
| Garlic | 3 | medium cloves, minced |
| Paprika | 1 | tablespoon |
| Mushrooms | ½ | pound, thinly sliced |
| Red bell pepper | 1 | small, slivered |
| Salt | ½ | teaspoon |
| Lowfat milk | 1½ | cups |
| Flour | 1 | tablespoon |
| Blue cheese | ¼ | pound, crumbled |
| Pepper | | A few grinds |
| Raw pecan pieces | ½ | cup |
| Fresh parsley, minced | ¼ | cup |
| Dried pasta | 1 | pound |

*Recommended pasta:* **sturdy tubes or spirals**

Trim the beans and cut at a slant into 1-inch pieces. Melt the butter in a high-walled skillet over low heat. Add the garlic and paprika and stir a bit. Add the beans, mushrooms, bell pepper, and salt. Stir and sauté 5 minutes, until mushrooms are limp and releasing their juices. Warm the milk in a small saucepan over low heat. Put several quarts of water on to boil for the pasta. Add the flour to the vegetables in the skillet and stir to distribute evenly. Add the warm milk, increase the heat to medium, and bring the sauce to a simmer. Add the blue cheese and pepper, and simmer gently 10 minutes while you cook the pasta until al dente. The sauce will thicken a little, but will have a rather thin consistency. Meanwhile, toast the pecans (see page 20) and chop finely. Stir half the pecans and half the parsley into the sauce. Drain the pasta briefly and toss in a warm bowl with the green bean sauce. Sprinkle the remaining pecans and parsley over the top. Serve very hot.

---

Each serving provides:

| 383 | Calories | 53 g | Carbohydrate |
| 14 g | Protein | 396 mg | Sodium |
| 13 g | Fat | 20 mg | Cholesterol |

---

# ✔ Pasta with Gorgonzola and Parmesan

*You can make this dish as a delicious main course for 4 people, or serve it as a starter for 8. Use a spinach pasta for a very pretty presentation.*

*Yield:* 8 side-dish servings

| | | |
|---|---|---|
| Butter | 3 | tablespoons |
| Garlic | 2 | medium cloves, minced |
| Gorgonzola cheese | 4 | ounces, crumbled |
| Lowfat milk | ½ | cup |
| Heavy cream | ⅓ | cup |
| Parmesan cheese, finely grated | ¾ | cup |
| Dried pasta | 1 | pound |

*Recommended pasta:* spinach fettuccine, lasagnette, or tagliatelle

Put several quarts of water on to boil for the pasta. Melt the butter in a large skillet and stir in the garlic. Heat just a bit, then add the Gorgonzola and milk; stir until smooth. Blend in the cream and just heat through. Cook the pasta until al dente, drain well, and add to the sauce in the skillet. Lift and toss gently to coat, then mix in the Parmesan. Transfer to a warm bowl and serve immediately.

---

### Each serving provides:

| | | | |
|---|---|---|---|
| 382 | Calories | 44 g | Carbohydrate |
| 15 g | Protein | 444 mg | Sodium |
| 16 g | Fat | 44 mg | Cholesterol |

---

# Baked and Stuffed Pasta

The appeal of casseroles is universal. Nearly every cuisine around the globe has developed unique dishes that are sauced and baked in the oven. In America—as in many other parts of the world—the classic casserole includes noodles and cheese. On this simple foundation, wonderful culinary masterpieces can be built.

A pretty and practical collection of baking dishes will inspire your efforts in this direction. Ovals, rectangles, and squares are the most commonly used shapes, though fun and unusual casseroles can be created in bundt pans or other molds.

There are a few hard and fast rules. Do preheat the oven so the casserole comes up to baking temperature quickly. Use a large pot with plenty of water to cook lasagna noodles. Be sure to include sufficient sauce so the finished product isn't dry and flavorless. Dishes that go into the oven with a cover on will have a uniform tender texture. To create a crunchy crust on top, remove the lid toward the end of the cooking time and let the casserole brown a bit. Allow casseroles to rest at room temperature 10–15 minutes so they can firm up before serving.

Many pasta cooks prefer to make sheets of dough from scratch for casseroles. If you don't wish to spend the time, dried lasagna and manicotti noodles are quite adequate. Try the homemade version some rainy Saturday when puttering in the kitchen feels just right.

As marvelous as they are when hot from the oven, casseroles magically improve with time. Store leftover casseroles covered in the refrigerator. Small amounts can be quickly reheated in a microwave or toaster oven for a delicious reprise. Many casseroles won't even require reheating—they can be enjoyed the following day at room temperature, or even cold. It's a matter of taste. You can also freeze most casseroles, whole or in individual servings, for a quick meal later.

Fillings for stuffed noodle preparations should be of a thick paste consistency; too runny and the pasta wrapper can become soggy during boiling. Again, you may wish to make fresh dough for stuffing, but fresh store-bought wonton wrappers make delicious ravioli. Look for them in the produce section of your supermarket or at Asian food stores.

A few of the recipes in this section start with commercially prepared stuffed pastas, such as tortellini and ravioli. Try a few different brands to discover the ones you like best. Keep some in the pantry or freezer for a quick pasta feast when time doesn't allow for from-scratch preparations.

Here we present our favorite baked and stuffed pastas. We hope they inspire you to create delectable new classics in your own kitchen.

# ✔ Burnt Butter and Wine Sauce for Ravioli

*Guy Hadler perfected this wonderfully simple dish. Use commercially prepared cheese ravioli or tortellini when an instant dinner is called for.*

*Yield:* 4 side-dish servings

| | | |
|---|---|---|
| **Butter** | 3 | tablespoons |
| **Garlic powder** | 1 | teaspoon |
| **White wine** | 1 | tablespoon |
| **Lemon juice** | ½ | teaspoon |
| **Fresh cheese ravioli or tortellini** | 8 | ounces |

Put several quarts of water on to boil for the ravioli. Meanwhile, melt the butter in a small cast-iron skillet over low heat. Add the garlic powder, wine, and lemon juice, turn off the heat, cover, and set aside. Cook the ravioli until tender, drain, and transfer to a warm serving bowl. Keep warm. Heat the butter mixture over high heat until it scorches, then turn the heat down to medium-high and reduce for a minute or two before drizzling it evenly over the ravioli. Serve immediately.

---

Each serving provides:

| 261 | Calories | 17 g | Carbohydrate |
|---|---|---|---|
| 9 g | Protein | 373 mg | Sodium |
| 17 g | Fat | 70 mg | Cholesterol |

---

# Spinach Eggplant Lasagna

*This Mediterranean-style lasagna has a wonderful flavor, light and fresh. And the layers create a beautiful color palette. As a variation, prepare it well ahead of time, let it cool, and serve small portions as appetizers.*

*Yield:* 10 main-course servings

### The sauce

| | | |
|---|---|---|
| Olive oil | 2 | tablespoons |
| Garlic | 2 | medium cloves, minced |
| Onion | 1 | medium, finely diced |
| Stewed tomatoes | 1 | 28-ounce can |
| Lemon | 2 | slices |
| Bay leaves | 3 | |
| Fresh basil leaves, minced | 3 | tablespoons |

### The casserole

| | | |
|---|---|---|
| Fresh spinach | 1 | bunch (about ¾ pound) |
| Eggplant | 1 | medium (about 1 pound) |
| Olive oil | 4 | tablespoons |
| Firm-style tofu | ¾ | pound |
| Part-skim ricotta cheese | 2½ | cups |
| Garlic | 3 | medium cloves, minced |
| Part-skim mozzarella cheese | 1 | pound, shredded |
| Green onions | 6 | sliced |
| Parmesan cheese, finely grated | ⅓ | cup |
| Dried lasagna noodles | 12 | ounces |

Preheat the oven to 350 degrees F. about 30 minutes before you are ready to bake the lasagna. To prepare the sauce, heat 2 tablespoons olive oil in a large pan and sauté the garlic and onion a couple of minutes. Add the tomatoes, lemon slices, bay leaves, and basil. Cook the sauce about 30 minutes, until it reduces slightly. Discard the lemon slices and bay leaves. Set aside.

Meanwhile, bring several quarts of water to a boil and cook the noodles until almost al dente. They will finish cooking in the oven. Cool the noodles in a large bowl of cold water that has a tablespoon of olive oil added. Drain and lay them on a tea towel to dry. Carefully wash the spinach, remove the stems, and place the leaves in a steamer rack over a couple of inches of boiling water in a lidded pot. Steam until it wilts. Place the cooked spinach in a colander to drain. Peel the eggplant and cut lengthwise into ½-inch-thick slices. Heat a little olive oil in a cast-iron skillet over medium heat and sauté the eggplant slices about 2 minutes per side until tender. This will need to be done in several batches, adding a little more olive oil each time (but don't exceed a total of 2 tablespoons of oil). Drain the cooked eggplant on paper towels until needed. Slice the tofu and blot with a tea towel to remove surface water. Mash it in a bowl with a potato masher or fork. Mix in the ricotta and garlic. Rub an 11 × 14-inch baking dish with 1 tablespoon olive oil. (If you do not have a dish this size you will have extra noodles, so hold out some of the other ingredients, which can be layered in a bread pan to create a second small casserole.) Layer the casserole as follows:

> half the tomato sauce
> layer of noodles
> all the eggplant slices
> ¾ of the mozzarella
> layer of noodles
> remainder of tomato sauce

ricotta-tofu mixture

spinach

green onions

remaining mozzarella

Parmesan

Cover and bake 30–40 minutes. Let stand 15 minutes before serving.

Each serving provides:

| | | | |
|---|---|---|---|
| 534 | Calories | 39 g | Carbohydrate |
| 33 g | Protein | 546 mg | Sodium |
| 27 g | Fat | 48 mg | Cholesterol |

*The Best 125 Meatless Pasta Dishes*

# Pasta al Pesto Frittata

*This unusual egg and pasta casserole comes together quickly. Serve it for brunch, lunch, or dinner, accompanied by a tangy salad or steamed vegetables.*

*Yield:* 8 side-dish servings

| | | |
|---|---|---|
| Olive oil | 1 | tablespoon |
| Eggs | 6 | large |
| Basil Pesto | ¼ | cup (see page 32) |
| Salt | | A scant pinch |
| Pepper | | A few grinds |
| Part-skim mozzarella cheese, shredded | ¾ | cup |
| Dried pasta | 6 | ounces |

*Recommended pasta:* linguine or spaghetti

Put a few quarts of water on to boil for the pasta. Preheat the oven to 375 degrees F. Rub the olive oil onto a heavy 10-inch skillet that can take the heat of the oven. Cook the pasta until al dente. Drain well. Distribute it in an even thickness over the bottom of the skillet and allow to cool 10 minutes. Meanwhile, whisk the eggs with the pesto, salt, and pepper, then stir in the cheese. Pour the egg mixture over the pasta, again being careful to distribute evenly. Bake uncovered 20 minutes, cut in wedges, and serve hot or at room temperature.

---

Each serving provides:

| | | | | |
|---|---|---|---|---|
| 209 | Calories | 18 g | Carbohydrate |
| 12 g | Protein | 158 mg | Sodium |
| 10 g | Fat | 167 mg | Cholesterol |

---

# Mexicali Lasagna

*Some traditional tamale pie ingredients are combined here to create a very unusual lasagna. It has been enjoyed by many friends, who were delightfully surprised by the green chilies and corn.*

*Yield:* 8 main-course servings

### The sauce

| | | |
|---|---|---|
| V-8 juice | 2 | cups |
| Lowfat milk | 1 | cup |
| Fresh cilantro, minced | ⅓ | cup, loosely packed |
| Dried oregano | 1 | tablespoon |
| Garlic powder | 1 | teaspoon |
| Flour | ¼ | cup |

### The casserole

| | | |
|---|---|---|
| Broccoli florets | 2 | cups, loosely packed |
| Canned whole green chilies | 1½ | cups, loosely packed |
| Olive oil | 1 | tablespoon |
| Part-skim ricotta cheese | 15 | ounces |
| Jalapeño jack cheese | 8 | ounces, shredded |
| Frozen corn | 1 | 10-ounce package |
| Parmesan cheese, finely grated | 2 | tablespoons |
| Dried lasagna noodles | 8 | ounces |

Well ahead of time, set the frozen corn out to thaw. Preheat the oven to 375 degrees F. about 30 minutes before you are ready to bake the lasagna. In a medium-size saucepan, heat the V-8 juice, milk, cilantro, oregano, and garlic powder. When this mixture is steaming hot, shake the flour in a small jar with ⅓ cup water until flour is incorporated. Whisk this roux into the sauce and simmer over low heat, whisking frequently, until slightly thickened, about 10 minutes.

Meanwhile, bring several quarts of water to a boil and cook noodles until almost tender. They will finish cooking in the oven. During the last 5 minutes of pasta cooking time, add the broccoli florets to the pot. Cool in cold water and drain, then lay noodles out in a single layer on a tea towel until needed. Set the broccoli aside. Clean the seeds and membranes from the chilies and slice into thin strips. Rub a 9 × 13-inch baking dish with 1 tablespoon olive oil. Ladle ½ cup sauce into the bottom and distribute evenly. Place a single layer of noodles over the sauce. Use half the chili strips to make a layer on top of the noodles. Use a soup spoon to dot the chilies with half the ricotta. Evenly distribute the broccoli florets and half the jack cheese over the ricotta. Spread with ¾ cup sauce and cover with another layer of noodles. Distribute the corn and the remaining chilies, ricotta, and jack cheese evenly over the noodles. Spread ¾ cup sauce evenly over these ingredients and top with a last layer of noodles. Distribute the remaining sauce over the lasagna and sprinkle evenly with the Parmesan. Cover and bake 45 minutes. Let stand 10 minutes before serving.

---

Each serving provides:

| 384 | Calories | 42 g | Carbohydrate |
|------|----------|--------|--------------|
| 21 g | Protein | 656 mg | Sodium |
| 15 g | Fat | 49 mg | Cholesterol |

---

# Baked Macaroni and Smoked Cheese

*Smoked gouda is particularly good for this dish, but smoked cheddar also yields delicious results. For good old all-American macaroni and cheese, use elbow-shaped noodles and substitute a mild cheddar for the smoked cheese.*

*Yield:* 8 main-course servings

| | | |
|---|---|---|
| Lowfat milk | 4 | cups |
| Butter | 3 | tablespoons plus 1 teaspoon |
| Onion | 1 | medium, coarsely chopped |
| Flour | 3 | tablespoons |
| Dry mustard | 1 | tablespoon |
| Cayenne pepper | ¼ | teaspoon |
| Smoked cheese | ½ | pound, shredded |
| Coarse dry bread crumbs | 1 | cup |
| Parmesan cheese, finely grated | ¼ | cup |
| Dried pasta | 1 | pound |

*Recommended pasta:* elbows, penne, or other tubes

Put several quarts of water on to boil for the pasta. Preheat oven to 375 degrees F. about 30 minutes before you are ready to bake the casserole. Warm the milk in a saucepan over very low heat. Melt 3 tablespoons of the butter over low heat in a separate heavy-bottomed saucepan or skillet. Add the onion and stir and sauté 3–4 minutes, until it begins to get limp. Add the flour and mustard and stir another minute or two, then stir in the warmed milk and cayenne. Turn the heat up to medium and cook 5–7 minutes. Add the smoked cheese and cook 3 minutes longer. The sauce will thicken slightly, but do not expect a really heavy sauce consistency. Meanwhile, cook the pasta until almost tender. You want the noodles to be still somewhat firm because they will finish cooking in the oven. Drain thoroughly. Rub a 3-quart baking dish with the remaining 1 teaspoon butter. In a large bowl, toss the pasta with the cheese sauce, then transfer to the baking dish. Combine the bread crumbs with the Parmesan and distribute this mixture evenly over the top of the casserole. Cover and bake 30 minutes, then remove cover and cook 5–10 minutes longer, until topping is crisp. Let stand at room temperature 10 minutes before serving.

| Each serving provides: | | | |
|---|---|---|---|
| 486 | Calories | 61 g | Carbohydrate |
| 22 g | Protein | 495 mg | Sodium |
| 16 g | Fat | 53 mg | Cholesterol |

# Savory Mushroom Custard with Pasta

*The flavors of this casserole suggest a light cream sauce with pesto, and the texture is melt-in-your-mouth smoothness. If you have a few cups of leftover cooked noodles on hand, this is a great way to use them. When made with spinach pasta in a clear glass dish, the presentation is particularly pretty.*

*Yield:* 8 main-course servings

| | | |
|---|---|---|
| Eggs | 6 | large |
| Butter | 3 | tablespoons |
| Mushrooms | 1 | pound, thinly sliced |
| Salt | ¾ | teaspoon |
| Pepper | | A few grinds |
| Basil Pesto | 3 | tablespoons (see page 32) |
| Lowfat milk | 3 | cups |
| Dried pasta | 8 | ounces |
| Olive oil (optional) | 1 | tablespoon |

*Recommended pasta:* spinach fettuccine or linguine, or 4 cups leftover cooked noodles

Preheat oven to 350 degrees F. about 30 minutes before you're ready to bake the casserole. Bring the eggs to room temperature. Unless you are using leftover noodles, cook pasta until al dente. If you are not yet ready to assemble the casserole, cool the pasta in cold water, drain, toss with a tablespoon of olive oil, and set aside. Melt the butter in a skillet. Add the mushrooms, sprinkle with ¼ teaspoon of the salt, and sauté about 8 minutes, until they have released their liquid and it has nearly evaporated. Add a little pepper and turn off the heat. Generously butter a 2-quart casserole or baking dish. In a bowl, whisk together the eggs, pesto, and the remaining ½ teaspoon salt. Warm the milk slightly in a small saucepan. Pour it into the egg mixture in a thin stream, gently whisking as you do so (milk must be only lukewarm, or it will cook the eggs). Make a layer of the noodles in the bottom of the casserole. Distribute the sautéed mushrooms over them. Evenly pour on the custard. Cover the casserole and place it in a larger baking pan that contains an inch or so of warm water. Put this arrangement into the oven and bake 45 minutes or so, until the custard is set. Let stand 10 minutes before serving.

---

Each serving provides:

| 290 | Calories | 30 g | Carbohydrate |
| 14 g | Protein | 378 mg | Sodium |
| 13 g | Fat | 173 mg | Cholesterol |

---

# Couscous Casserole with Capers and Tarragon

*How many years has it been since you made a casserole for guests? This recipe will open the door to a whole new realm of "meal in a dish" options. A side dish of steamed vegetables and a leafy salad is all you need to round it out. Your company will enjoy the flavors, and you will enjoy the ease of preparation and serving.*

*Yield:* 6 main-course servings

| | | |
|---|---|---|
| Olive oil | 4 | tablespoons |
| Onion | 1 | medium, finely diced |
| Red bell pepper | 1 | medium, finely diced |
| Capers, drained, minced | 4 | teaspoons |
| Fresh parsley, minced | ¾ | cup, loosely packed |
| Garlic | 2 | medium cloves, minced |
| Dried tarragon | 2 | teaspoons |
| Hot water | 2 | cups |
| Dried couscous | 1 | cup |
| Lowfat milk | 1 | cup |
| Eggs | 3 | large |
| Parmesan cheese, finely grated | ¾ | cup |

Preheat the oven to 350 degrees F. about 30 minutes before you're ready to bake the casserole. Heat 3 tablespoons of the olive oil in a 2-quart saucepan and gently sauté the onion, bell pepper, capers, parsley, garlic, and tarragon a couple of minutes. Add hot water and the couscous, bring to a boil, then cover and remove from the heat. Let stand 10 minutes. Whisk together the milk and eggs and add this and the Parmesan to the couscous mixture. Combine well. Use the remaining tablespoon of olive oil to coat a 2-quart casserole dish. Pour in the couscous mixture, cover, and bake 30 minutes.

---

Each serving provides:

| 319 | Calories | 29 g | Carbohydrate |
| 14 g | Protein | 336 mg | Sodium |
| 16 g | Fat | 118 mg | Cholesterol |

---

# Curried Couscous Casserole

*Couscous is one of the least common pastas, but once you discover it you will begin to crave it. The texture is much different than that of other pastas, more akin to a grain. It is easy to prepare and will be complemented by many different seasonings.*

*Yield:* 6 main-course servings

| | | |
|---|---|---|
| Water | 2½ | cups |
| Low-sodium vegetable broth cube | 1 | |
| Dried couscous | 1 | cup |
| Olive oil | 3 | tablespoons |
| Red bell pepper | 1 | medium, diced |
| Green onions | 2 | minced |
| Peas, fresh or frozen | 1 | cup |
| Cooked garbanzo beans | 1⅓ | cups |
| Dried tomatoes, minced | 2 | tablespoons |
| Curry powder | 1 | tablespoon |
| Salt | ¼ | teaspoon |
| Lowfat milk | ¾ | cup |
| Fresh cilantro, minced | ¼ | cup |

*Optional garnishes:* **lemon wedges, light sour cream, plain lowfat yogurt**

Preheat oven to 350 degrees F. about 30 minutes before you are ready to bake the casserole. Heat the water and the vegetable broth cube to a boil in a 2-quart saucepan that has a tight-fitting lid. Stir in the couscous. Remove from the heat, cover, and let stand about 15 minutes. Heat 2 tablespoons of the olive oil in a small skillet over low heat. Sauté the bell pepper and green onions a minute or two. Stir in the peas, garbanzo beans, dried tomatoes, curry powder, and salt. Heat through. Stir in the milk. Mix all of this, along with the cilantro, into the couscous, blending well. Use the remaining tablespoon of olive oil to coat a 1½-quart casserole dish. Pour in the couscous mixture, cover, and bake 30 minutes. Serve with lemon wedges and yogurt or sour cream, if desired.

Each serving provides:

| | | | |
|---|---|---|---|
| 278 | Calories | 42 g | Carbohydrate |
| 11 g | Protein | 151 mg | Sodium |
| 8 g | Fat | 1 mg | Cholesterol |

# Sauce of Mushrooms, Spinach, and Capers for Tortellini

*Our friend Lori Shull created this wonderful dish. The sauce is rich, creamy, and well balanced. She usually serves it as a main course, but has also put it out with toothpicks as an appetizer.*

*Yield:* 4 main-course servings

| | | |
|---|---|---|
| Neufchâtel cheese | 6 | ounces |
| Frozen chopped spinach | 6 | ounces |
| Butter | 1 | tablespoon |
| Red bell pepper | 1 | large, diced |
| Onion | 1 | medium, diced |
| Mushrooms | ¼ | pound, thickly sliced |
| Garlic | 2 | medium cloves, minced |
| Tomato | 1 | medium, diced |
| White wine | ¼ | cup |
| Parmesan cheese, finely grated | ¼ | cup |
| Capers, drained, minced | 1½ | tablespoons |
| Dried oregano | ½ | teaspoon |
| Dried basil | ½ | teaspoon |
| Fresh cheese tortellini | 12 | ounces |

Set the Neufchâtel cheese out well ahead of time to bring it to room temperature. Thaw the spinach and drain well. Put several quarts of water on to boil for the tortellini. Melt the butter in a large skillet over low heat. Add the bell pepper, onion, mushrooms, and garlic and sauté several minutes. Add the Neufchâtel, spinach, tomato, and wine. Blend well. Mix in the

Parmesan, capers, oregano, and basil. Continue to cook until the mixture just begins to simmer, stirring constantly. Meanwhile, cook the tortellini until tender. Drain well and add to the sauce. Toss to coat and heat through. Serve in a warm bowl.

Each serving provides:

| | | | |
|---|---|---|---|
| 464 | Calories | 49 g | Carbohydrate |
| 23 g | Protein | 812 mg | Sodium |
| 19 g | Fat | 92 mg | Cholesterol |

# Acorn Squash Ravioli with Rosemary Walnut Sauce

*This is a dish to make on a rainy Saturday afternoon. Ravioli preparation is rather time-consuming, particularly when making dough from scratch, but the results are always worth it. Make more than you need and freeze them.*

*Yield:* 6 main-course servings

### The filling

| | | |
|---|---|---|
| Acorn squash | 1¼ | pounds |
| Butter | 2 | tablespoons |
| Lowfat milk | 1 | cup |
| Half-and-half | ½ | cup |
| Freshly grated nutmeg | ⅛ | teaspoon |
| Ground cinnamon | ¼ | teaspoon |
| Salt and pepper | | To taste |
| Honey | 1 | teaspoon |
| Basic egg noodles | 1 | recipe (see page 16) |

### The sauce

| | | |
|---|---|---|
| Raw walnuts, chopped | ½ | cup |
| Butter | 3 | tablespoons |
| Rosemary Pesto | 2 | tablespoons (see page 33) |

Peel and chop the squash; you should have about 3½ cups. Place the butter and ¼ cup water in a large skillet. When the butter melts, add the squash and cook over low heat until tender, stirring occasionally, about 30 minutes. Remove from heat and mash with a potato masher. Return to the heat and stir in the milk and half-and-half. Cook, stirring frequently, about 20 minutes. Stir in the nutmeg, cinnamon, salt, pepper, and honey.

Prepare the pasta dough as called for in the recipe. Roll out by hand, or save time by using a pasta machine, following the manufacturer's directions. Lay out strips of pasta about 2 inches wide and 10 inches long, in pairs. On one of each pair of noodles place about a teaspoon of the squash filling every 1½ inches, going the length of the pasta. Put a few drops of water on your finger and draw a square around each mound of filling to moisten the dough. Cover the entire strip with another noodle and press the dough down firmly with your fingers to seal around each mound, pushing out any air as you do this. Slice through the dough to create individual ravioli. Continue this process until all the filling and dough are used up. As you complete them, wrap the ravioli in a lightly floured tea towel until ready to cook, so they do not dry out. Meanwhile, heat several quarts of water to a rapid boil and add a tablespoon of oil. Cook the ravioli 5–8 minutes, until tender.

While they are cooking, gently toast the chopped walnuts (see page 20). Melt the butter in a small pan and add the Rosemary Pesto; heat through. Serve the ravioli on warm plates drizzled with the sauce. Sprinkle with the walnuts.

---

Each serving provides:

| 482 | Calories | 49 g | Carbohydrate |
|-----|----------|------|--------------|
| 13 g | Protein | 364 mg | Sodium |
| 27 g | Fat | 142 mg | Cholesterol |

---

# Spinach Nutmeg Ravioli with Tomato and Brandy Cream

*This is really a shortcut ravioli recipe because the noodle is the commercially prepared fresh round wonton wrapper. You can also make this dish with fresh homemade pasta, if you have an abundance of time.*

*Yield:* 6 main-course servings

### The sauce

| | | |
|---|---|---|
| Tomato sauce | 1 | 16-ounce can |
| Half-and-half | 1 | cup |
| Freshly grated nutmeg | ⅛ | teaspoon |
| Brandy | ¼ | cup |

### The filling

| | | |
|---|---|---|
| Frozen chopped spinach | 10 | ounces |
| Butter | 3 | tablespoons |
| Onion | 1 | small, finely diced |
| Garlic | 2 | medium cloves, minced |
| Freshly grated nutmeg | ⅛ | teaspoon |
| Lowfat milk | ¼ | cup |
| Part-skim ricotta cheese | 8 | ounces |
| Fresh round wonton wrappers | 12 | ounces |

Ahead of time, thaw the spinach and drain well. Combine the tomato sauce, half-and-half, and ⅛ teaspoon nutmeg in a skillet. Bring to a simmer and cook about 10 minutes, stirring often. Add the brandy and heat through, then set aside.

To make the filling, melt the butter in a skillet and sauté the onion, garlic, and ⅛ teaspoon nutmeg 2–3 minutes. Stir in the spinach and milk. Add the ricotta, mixing well. Turn off the heat.

To assemble the ravioli, place a wonton wrapper on a floured work surface. Place a scant teaspoonful of the spinach mixture on one side. Dip your finger in water and draw a line around the outer edge of the noodle. Fold over and seal tightly, pressing out any trapped air as you go. Wrap the filled ravioli in a lightly floured tea towel so they do not dry out. Continue this process until you have filled all the wrappers. Bring several quarts of water to a boil and cook the ravioli until tender. Briefly reheat the sauce while they are cooking. Serve the ravioli on heated plates with the sauce drizzled over the top.

| | Each serving provides: | | |
|---|---|---|---|
| 379 | Calories | 43 g | Carbohydrate |
| 15 g | Protein | 635 mg | Sodium |
| 14 g | Fat | 42 mg | Cholesterol |

# Oregano Pesto Manicotti

*Oregano pesto has a flavor all its own. It is worth making for this dish, but you can substitute basil pesto if you have some on hand. The presentation is festive and the flavors a delight.*

*Yield:* 6 main-course servings

**The sauce**

| | | |
|---|---|---|
| Olive oil | 2 | tablespoons |
| Garlic | 2 | medium cloves, minced |
| Onion | 1 | medium, diced |
| Stewed tomatoes | 1 | 28-ounce can |
| Fresh oregano leaves | 2 | tablespoons |
| Lemon | 2 | slices |
| Bay leaves | 3 | |
| Port | 2 | tablespoons |

**The filling**

| | | |
|---|---|---|
| Firm-style tofu | 6 | ounces |
| Part-skim ricotta cheese | 1 | cup |
| Light sour cream | ¾ | cup |
| Egg | 1 | large, beaten |
| Oregano Pesto | 1 | cup (see page 36) |
| Part-skim mozzarella cheese, shredded | 1 | cup |
| Parmesan cheese, finely grated | ½ | cup |
| Olive oil | 1 | tablespoon |
| Dried manicotti noodles | 8 | ounces |

Preheat the oven to 350 degrees F. about 30 minutes before you are ready to bake the manicotti. Heat 2 tablespoons olive oil in a large pan and sauté the garlic and onion several minutes. Add the tomatoes, oregano, lemon slices, and bay leaves. Cook over medium-high heat about 30 minutes, stirring occasionally. Reduce the heat and add the port. Cook about 15 minutes longer, until the sauce is rather thick. Turn off the heat and set aside.

Meanwhile, cook the manicotti noodles in a very large pot of water until almost al dente. They need lots of room to swim around while cooking, so prepare in two batches if necessary. The noodles must be undercooked in order to stuff them. They will finish cooking in the oven. Drain and rinse the noodles and lay them on a tea towel to dry. Slice the tofu and blot with a tea towel to remove surface moisture. Mash in a large bowl with a potato masher or fork. Add the ricotta, sour cream, egg, and pesto. Combine well. Add the mozzarella and Parmesan and stir to incorporate. Stuff each noodle with the cheese mixture; a baby spoon works well for this. Rub a 9 × 13-inch baking dish with 1 tablespoon olive oil. Arrange the stuffed manicotti in the pan in a single layer. Spoon the tomato sauce over them along their center and bake, covered, 35 minutes.

---

Each serving provides:

| | | | |
|---|---|---|---|
| 676 | Calories | 47 g | Carbohydrate |
| 30 g | Protein | 486 mg | Sodium |
| 42 g | Fat | 72 mg | Cholesterol |

---

# Tofu Pesto Rollups

*In this dish the noodles are rolled up jelly-roll fashion, which makes a very nice presentation with the multicolored fillings and the curly edges of the noodles. If you are short of time, you can substitute a store-bought marinara sauce for the Tomato Sauce with Fresh Oregano. For this dish, avoid whole wheat lasagna varieties as they break apart too easily. Be sure to gauge the amount of filling in each rollup carefully, so you will have enough for 12 noodles (you may wish to cook a few extra noodles, in case some break).*

*Yield:* 8 main-course servings

| | | |
|---|---|---|
| Firm-style tofu | 6 | ounces |
| Part-skim ricotta cheese | 1 | cup |
| Light sour cream | ½ | cup |
| Basil Pesto | ½ | cup (see page 32) |
| Garlic | 3 | medium cloves, minced |
| Olive oil | 1 | tablespoon |
| Tomato Sauce with Fresh Oregano | 1½ | cups (see page 176) |
| Parmesan cheese, finely grated | ½ | cup |
| Dried semolina lasagna noodles | 12 | ounces |

Preheat the oven to 350 degrees F. Bring a large pan of water to a boil for the noodles, as they need plenty of room to swim around in while cooking. Cook the noodles until almost tender. They will finish cooking as they bake. Remove very gently from the water, rinse under cold water, drain well, and place on a tea towel to dry. (You want to remove as much of the water as possible.) Slice the tofu and blot with a tea towel to remove surface water. Mash it in a mixing bowl with a fork or potato masher.

Add the ricotta, sour cream, pesto, and garlic and combine thoroughly. Spread about a ¼-inch layer of the mixture along the entire length and width of each noodle and roll up. Rub a 9 × 13-inch baking dish with the olive oil. Place the rollups in the dish seam side down. Top them with the sauce and Parmesan. Bake uncovered for 25 minutes and serve immediately.

| Each serving provides: | | | |
|---|---|---|---|
| 429 | Calories | 45 g | Carbohydrate |
| 20 g | Protein | 414 mg | Sodium |
| 20 g | Fat | 23 mg | Cholesterol |

# Pesto Ricotta Shells with Herbed Tomato Sauce

*These jumbo shells look so charming when they are served, and they taste wonderful!*

*Yield:* 6 main-course servings

### The sauce

| | | |
|---|---|---|
| Fresh pear tomatoes | 1½ | pounds |
| Olive oil | 1 | tablespoon |
| Onion | 1 | small, minced |
| Garlic | 2 | medium cloves, minced |
| Lemon | 1 | slice |
| Fresh oregano leaves | 1 | tablespoon |
| Fresh chives, minced | 1 | tablespoon |
| White wine | ½ | cup |

### The filling

| | | |
|---|---|---|
| Egg | 1 | large |
| Part-skim ricotta cheese | 1 | cup |
| Basil Pesto | 1 | cup (see page 32) |
| Parmesan cheese, finely grated | ½ | cup |
| Dried jumbo pasta shells | 8 | ounces |

Preheat the oven to 350 degrees F. about 30 minutes before you are ready to bake the shells. Blanch, peel, and seed the tomatoes (see page 20) and chop coarsely. Heat the olive oil in a large pan and sauté the onion and garlic a minute or two. Add the tomatoes and lemon. Simmer over low heat 15 minutes, then crush the tomatoes with a wooden spoon and stir in the herbs and wine. Continue to cook until reduced to a thick sauce consistency.

Bring several quarts of water to a boil. Add a little olive oil and cook the shells until almost tender, stirring frequently so they do not stick to the bottom of the pan or each other. They will finish cooking in the oven. Lift them into a colander and rinse with cold water. Drain well. Beat the egg and whisk in the ricotta and pesto. Stir in the Parmesan. Spoon half the tomato sauce into a 9 × 13-inch baking dish. Fill each shell with some of the ricotta mixture and place in the baking dish. Spoon remaining sauce over them, bake uncovered 20 minutes, and serve immediately.

---

Each serving provides:

| | | | |
|---|---|---|---|
| 531 | Calories | 46 g | Carbohydrate |
| 23 g | Protein | 458 mg | Sodium |
| 29 g | Fat | 64 mg | Cholesterol |

---

# Shells Filled with Dried Tomatoes and Pesto

*This dish is wonderful for a summer party. The shells are served at room temperature so the oven does not heat up the kitchen. Or serve them during the winter holiday season as an appetizer. The red and green colors fit in perfectly with that time of year.*

*Yield:* 8 main-course servings

| | | |
|---|---|---|
| Neufchâtel cheese | 16 | ounces |
| Olive oil | 1 | tablespoon |
| Firm-style tofu | 4 | ounces |
| Part-skim ricotta cheese | 1 | cup |
| Garlic | 4 | medium cloves, minced |
| Basil Pesto | ¾ | cup (see page 32) |
| Dried tomatoes, minced | ½ | cup |
| Salt and pepper | | To taste |
| Pine nuts | ½ | cup |
| Fresh parsley (for garnish) | | Many sprigs |
| Dried jumbo pasta shells | 32–36 | |

Well ahead of time, set the Neufchâtel cheese out to bring it to room temperature. Bring several quarts of water with a little oil in it to a boil and cook the shells until al dente, stirring frequently so they do not stick to the bottom of the pan or to each other. Drain well. Refill the pan with cold water and add the olive oil, then stir in the cooked pasta to cool. The olive oil will prevent the shells from sticking together. When cool, drain again and gently shake to remove all the water. Set shells aside to dry on a tea towel.

Meanwhile, slice the tofu and blot the slices with a tea towel to remove surface water. Mash it in a bowl with a potato masher or fork. Mix in the Neufchâtel cheese, ricotta, garlic, pesto, and dried tomatoes until creamy in texture. Season with salt and pepper. Toast the pine nuts (see page 20). To stuff the shells, hold open in the palm of your hand and spoon in the filling. Arrange the filled shells on a serving platter. Top each one with a couple of pine nuts and a parsley sprig. Refrigerate several hours. Bring to room temperature before serving.

| Each serving provides: | | | |
|---|---|---|---|
| 591 | Calories | 50 g | Carbohydrate |
| 25 g | Protein | 408 mg | Sodium |
| 35 g | Fat | 58 mg | Cholesterol |

# Spinach Lasagna with Port

*This lasagna is fairly traditional in flavor and composition, except for the subtle accent of the port. Prepare this dish when you are feeding a crowd, as everything can be done ahead. Add garlic bread and a big green salad and you are ready to feast. Lasagna also freezes well, so one pan of this could be put away for a future meal.*

*Yield:* 16 main-dish servings

**The sauce**

| | | |
|---|---|---|
| Olive oil | 3 | tablespoons |
| Onions | 2 | medium, coarsely chopped |
| Celery, diced | 1 | cup |
| Garlic | 3 | medium cloves, minced |
| Chopped black olives | 1 | 4½-ounce can |
| Lemon | 2 | slices |
| Crushed tomatoes | 2 | 28-ounce cans |
| Dried oregano | 1 | tablespoon |
| Dried basil | 1 | tablespoon |
| Bay leaves | 4 | |
| Salt | ¼ | teaspoon |
| Pepper | ⅛ | teaspoon |
| Port | ¾ | cup |

**The filling**

| | | |
|---|---|---|
| Fresh spinach | 2 | bunches (about 1½ pounds) |
| Firm-style tofu | 6 | ounces |
| Part-skim ricotta cheese | 2½ | cups |
| Light sour cream | 1 | cup |
| Eggs | 3 | large, beaten |

| | | |
|---|---|---|
| Fresh parsley, minced | 1 | cup |
| Dried oregano | 1 | tablespoon |
| Dried basil | 1 | tablespoon |
| Salt and pepper | | to taste |
| Part-skim mozzarella cheese, shredded | 3½ | cups |
| Parmesan cheese, finely grated | 1 | cup |
| Dried lasagna noodles | 1 | pound |
| Olive oil | 2 | tablespoons |

Preheat the oven to 350 degrees F. about 30 minutes before you are ready to bake the lasagna. Heat the olive oil in a large pan and sauté the onion, celery, and garlic a few minutes. Add the olives, lemon slices, and tomatoes, then stir in the oregano, basil, bay leaves, salt, and pepper. Simmer over low heat 30–40 minutes, stirring occasionally. Add the port during the last 15 minutes of cooking.

While the sauce is cooking you can prepare the filling. Carefully wash the spinach, remove the stems, and place the leaves in a steamer rack over a couple of inches of boiling water in a lidded pot. Steam until it wilts. Place the cooked spinach in a colander to cool. Squeeze to remove as much water as possible; set aside. Slice the tofu and blot with a tea towel to remove surface water. Mash the tofu in a mixing bowl with a fork or potato masher. Stir in the ricotta, sour cream, eggs, parsley, oregano, basil, salt, and pepper and combine well. Bring a huge quantity of water to a boil in a very large pot and cook the noodles until almost al dente. (Lasagna noodles need lots of room to swim around freely as they cook, so if you don't have a huge pot, cook them in batches.) The noodles will finish cooking in the oven. Cool them in a bowl of cold water, drain, and place on a tea towel until you need them. Oil two 9 × 13-inch glass baking dishes with 1 tablespoon olive oil each. Layer the ingredients as follows: sauce, noodles, spinach, ricotta mixture, noodles, mozzarella, sauce, Parmesan. Cover with foil and bake 45 minutes. Remove the foil and bake 5 minutes longer. The sauce should be bubbling hot and the top slightly brown. Let stand about 10 minutes before cutting.

---

Each serving provides:

| | | | |
|---|---|---|---|
| 358 | Calories | 34 g | Carbohydrate |
| 22 g | Protein | 591 mg | Sodium |
| 15 g | Fat | 71 mg | Cholesterol |

---

*The Best 125 Meatless Pasta Dishes*

# Porcini, Mustard, and Ricotta Ravioli with Lemon Oregano Cream

*Making ravioli from scratch is a labor of love and dinner guests are sure to be impressed by your devotion. If you aren't interested in practicing this art, you can use fresh wonton wrappers from the supermarket. Homemade is preferable, but either way the flavors of the filling and the sauce make for a very special meal.*

*Yield:* 6 main-course servings

### The filling

| | | |
|---|---|---|
| Dried porcini mushrooms | 1 | ounce |
| Mustard greens | 1 | bunch (about ¾ pound) |
| Butter | 2 | tablespoons |
| Garlic | 3 | medium cloves, minced |
| Fresh oregano leaves | 1 | tablespoon |
| Part-skim ricotta cheese | 1 | cup |
| Salt | ½ | teaspoon |
| Pepper | | Several grinds |
| Basic egg noodles | 1 | recipe (see page 16) |
| Olive oil | 1 | tablespoon |

**The sauce**

| | |
|---|---|
| Sesame seeds | 1 tablespoon |
| Butter | 2 tablespoons |
| Salt | ¼ teaspoon |
| Lemon juice | 2 tablespoons |
| Half-and-half | ½ cup |
| Flour | 1 tablespoon |
| Fresh oregano leaves | 1 tablespoon |

Soak the porcini in 2 cups hot water for 30 minutes or so. Lift out the mushrooms. Strain the soaking liquid through a paper coffee filter to remove any grit and set aside. Coarsely chop the mushrooms. Wash and dry the mustard greens, chop coarsely, and set aside. In a high-walled skillet, melt the butter over low heat. Add the garlic and 1 tablespoon fresh oregano. Stir and sauté a minute or two, then add the chopped mushrooms. Stir and sauté 3–4 minutes longer, then add the mustard greens all at once, along with 2 tablespoons of mushroom soaking liquid. Put a tight lid on the pot and cook over low heat 7–8 minutes, until greens are wilted and tender. Spoon this mixture into a food processor and pulse to chop finely, or mince by hand. In a bowl, stir this mixture into the ricotta. Add the salt and pepper, and stir again to distribute everything evenly.

Prepare the dough as called for in the recipe. Roll out by hand, or save time by using a pasta machine, following the manufacturer's directions. Lay out strips of pasta about 2 inches wide and 10 inches long, in pairs. On one of each pair of noodles, place about a teaspoon of the filling every 1½ inches, going the length of the pasta. Put a few drops of water on your finger and draw a square around each mound of filling to moisten the dough. Cover the entire strip with another noodle and press the dough down firmly with your fingers to seal around each mound, pushing out any air as you do this. Slice through the dough to create individual ravioli. Continue this process until all the filling and dough are used up. As you complete

*The Best 125 Meatless Pasta Dishes*

them, wrap the ravioli in a lightly floured tea towel until ready to cook, so they do not dry out. Meanwhile, bring several quarts of water to a rapid boil and add a tablespoon of oil. Cook the ravioli 6–8 minutes, until tender.

While they are cooking, toast the sesame seeds (see page 20) and set aside. Heat 1 cup of the mushroom soaking liquid with the butter and salt in a small saucepan over low heat. When simmering, whisk in the lemon juice, then the half-and-half. Vigorously shake the flour with 3 tablespoons water in a small lidded jar. When the sauce is again simmering, whisk in the flour and water mixture. Simmer and whisk over medium heat about 5 minutes, until sauce thickens a little. Turn off the heat and stir in the oregano. Serve the ravioli very hot with a bit of the sauce drizzled over them. Sprinkle with toasted sesame seeds to provide a nice light crunch.

Each serving provides:

| 413 | Calories | 46 g | Carbohydrate |
|---|---|---|---|
| 16 g | Protein | 641 mg | Sodium |
| 19 g | Fat | 147 mg | Cholesterol |

# Garden Basket Lasagna

*This lasagna is just like Mom used to make, but without the meat! The flavors are pure and simple and the texture rich and cheesy. To keep the sodium level of this dish reasonable, be sure to use a salt-free variety of canned tomatoes.*

*Yield:* 8 main-course servings

### The sauce

| | | |
|---|---|---|
| Olive oil | 3 | tablespoons |
| Onions | 3 | medium, coarsely chopped |
| Garlic | 3 | medium cloves, minced |
| Tomato paste | 2 | 6-ounce cans |
| Low-sodium whole tomatoes | 2 | 28-ounce cans |
| Fresh parsley, minced | 1 | cup |
| Dried oregano | 2 | teaspoons |
| Dried basil | 2 | teaspoons |
| Bay leaves | 3 | |
| Lemon | 2 | slices |
| Salt | ¼ | teaspoon |
| Pepper | | A few grinds |

### The filling

| | | |
|---|---|---|
| Caraway seeds | 1 | tablespoon |
| Part-skim ricotta cheese | 15 | ounces |
| Light sour cream | 1 | cup |
| Olive oil | 1 | tablespoon |
| Zucchini | 2 | medium, thinly sliced |
| Yellow squash | 2 | medium, thinly sliced |
| Green bell pepper | 2 | medium, thinly sliced |

*The Best 125 Meatless Pasta Dishes*

| Part-skim mozzarella cheese | 8 | ounces, shredded |
| Parmesan cheese, finely grated | ½ | cup |
| | | |
| Dried lasagna noodles | 8 | ounces |
| Olive oil | 1 | tablespoon |

About 30 minutes before baking, preheat the oven to 350 degrees F. Heat the olive oil in a large skillet and sauté the onions and garlic several minutes. Add the tomato paste and chopped canned tomatoes, discarding the juice drained from one of the cans, but including the juice from the other. Bring to a simmer and add the parsley, oregano, basil, bay leaves, lemon slices, salt, and pepper. Simmer uncovered over low heat about 1 hour, stirring occasionally, until the sauce is considerably reduced. Meanwhile, bring several quarts of water to a boil and cook the pasta until almost al dente. It will finish cooking in the oven. Cool the noodles in a bowl of cold water, drain, and place on a tea towel to dry until you need them.

Toast the caraway seeds (see page 20) and mix them with the ricotta and sour cream. Rub a 9 × 13-inch baking dish with 1 tablespoon olive oil. Put ¼ of the tomato sauce on the bottom, then add a layer of sliced vegetables, then a layer of noodles. Dot with some of the ricotta mixture and sprinkle on some mozzarella. Repeat the layers 2 or 3 times. Top with the Parmesan. Cover with foil and bake 45 minutes. Uncover and bake 10 minutes longer. Let stand at room temperature 10 minutes before serving.

---

Each serving provides:

| 443 | Calories | 50 g | Carbohydrate |
| 24 g | Protein | 750 mg | Sodium |
| 18 g | Fat | 38 mg | Cholesterol |

---

# Cooking Up a Healthier Planet

Perhaps you feel you've heard enough about saving the planet. You may have read all the books and magazines, seen all the programs on television. Perhaps you think you know it all.

But just knowing isn't enough. Are you feeling it yet—outrage at the abuses, grief at the losses, righteous determination to help preserve what's left of the diversity and integrity of our ecosystem?

Many of us have chosen to avoid the issues—closed our minds and hearts to the barrage of data. Too much bad news, too many overwhelming challenges, too painful! What, after all, can we do about it?

Well, here comes the good news. Massive healing is made of minuscule changes. Every decision we make as consumers, every discussion we have with friends, all of our smallest and most mundane habits make a difference. Like cells in this huge living organism called Earth, every word or act—every choice—is either diseased or healthy, part of the problem or part of the solution.

So cooks, take heart and take responsibility. Let's make our choices—at the market, in the kitchen, in the garden— healthy ones. Here are just a few ways we as cooks can help save the world:

- Buy organic. The statistics on pesticide-related pollution of our air, water, and food are horrifying. We don't yet know the cumulative effect of a lifetime of eating chemical-laden foods—those of us now living are guinea pigs—but the preliminary signs are not encouraging. There is no question that pesticides are unhealthy for our bodies and for the planet. Demonstrate your concern and commitment by paying a little extra for organic produce. Request that your grocer carry organic foods. It is only through widespread consumer demand that we will see healthier farming practices and lower organic food prices. Better yet, have fun growing your own organic food, or buy from local organic farmers.

- Eat low on the food chain. There are health risks associated with meat eating beyond the much-publicized heart disease connection. About half of the 25 million pounds of antibiotics produced in the United States annually is fed to livestock, and residues remain in the meat you see in the supermarket case. In addition, salmonella contamination is found in almost 40 percent of all poultry, 12 percent of pork, and 5 percent of beef in the United States.

From an environmental perspective, consider that it takes between 22 and 44 times less fossil fuel to produce beans and grains than to produce meat. In addition, an estimated 85 percent of our topsoil erosion is associated with raising livestock.

If you have humanitarian leanings, you will be impressed by statistics suggesting that vastly more people can be fed from an acre of land devoted to grain cultivation rather than livestock grazing. There are other ethical concerns to consider—for instance, many people consciously demonstrate their respect for all life by declining to eat animals.

Whatever your stand on these challenging issues, it makes sense for your health and the planet's health to switch to a grain- and vegetable-based diet—including lots of meatless pasta!

- Minimize or eliminate packaging: pre-cycle. The first simple step is to purchase a basket or cloth bag for carrying groceries home. Plastic bags won't decompose in the landfill, and the ink used to print on them emits dangerous toxins when burned. Paper bags are biodegradable, but not a truly responsible option because they're made from trees. Choosing paper over plastic packaging is good, but buying food in bulk and taking it home in your own containers (like reused glass jars) is much better.

- Buy unbleached paper products—and minimize their use. White paper used to make coffee filters, paper towels, toilet paper, and the like is bleached, and the bleaching process creates dioxin, a deadly toxin now polluting our water. Rethink your consumption of plastic wraps. They are laden with potentially harmful chemicals that may leach into food, and they linger a long time in the landfill. Store food in the refrigerator in reusable containers. Clean up with rags instead of paper towels. Use wax paper, which is biodegradable, instead of plastic or foil when disposable wraps are unavoidable.

- Conserve energy in the kitchen. Check the temperature of your refrigerator and freezer—just a few degrees colder than necessary can substantially increase your energy consumption. Refrigerator temperature should be between 38 and 42 degrees Fahrenheit, the freezer between 0 and 5 degrees Fahrenheit. When you shop for a gas range, remember that an electronic ignition system will use about 40 percent less gas than a pilot light. Use a pipe cleaner to keep gas ports unclogged on your burners. For reheating items or baking small quantities, use a toaster oven rather than your larger oven. Better yet, invest in a solar box cooker. They're simple to build from inexpensive materials and they cook food absolutely free of charge. The environment also pays no price when we let the sun do the cooking. For more information, contact Solar Box Cookers International, 1724 11th St., Sacramento, CA 95814; telephone (916) 444-6616; fax (916) 447-8689.

- Don't waste water. The story of water use and abuse, and their effects on our ecosystem is complex. Here, suffice it to say that when we waste water in our homes we contribute to chemical pollution and to the need for dams, which have a very serious impact on the health of our rivers and land. Kitchens are, by nature, water intensive. We need to wash most foods, we cook many foods in water, and we use great quantities of the stuff in cleaning up after meals. This doesn't include the water we simply drink—perhaps the most justifiable of all our water uses. If you grow some of your own food, your garden is another heavy water consumer.

  There are many simple steps you can take to reduce your garden and kitchen water consumption. First and foremost, don't turn on the tap and simply let water flow down the drain. Fill a bowl or bucket with water and use it to wash vegetables, rather than running the tap. This "gray water" can be used again, with the addition of soap, for washing dishes or wiping down counters and floors. Collect all water you use in the kitchen that has not been salted or harshly soaped and water plants with it. (Pasta cooking water can be recycled this way only if you choose not to salt the pot.) When cleaning up, wash and rinse in basins instead of letting the water flow. Another great water saver is to cool foods by placing them in a bowl of cold, even iced, water rather than letting cold tap water run over them. This is an excellent method for stopping the cooking of pasta, vegetables, and the like, if you do not want to keep them warm after cooking. Then you can reuse the water in the garden or for some other purpose.

- Minimize garbage production. We Americans are a wasteful lot, encouraged by the throwaway ethic of a consumer society. In many parts of the country, however, the seriousness of garbage proliferation is painfully apparent. Landfills are loaded and there simply isn't any place for the garbage to go. Fortunately, we can have a great deal of impact on this situation. Recycling has caught on nationwide as a method for reducing solid waste, while at the same time saving on the cost of producing new packaging materials. If the sanitation department of your city or town doesn't yet offer curbside recycling, bring pressure to bear on the policymakers so it will be instituted. Meanwhile, do some research to discover whether there are companies nearby that buy recycled materials and get together with your neighbors to collect them. It is possible you could earn a little money by gathering recyclables and transporting them to the collection site. Newspapers and other paper products, aluminum and tin cans, glass of all types, waxed milk cartons, and many types of plastic—even Styrofoam—can be recycled in many areas.

Kitchen food scraps constitute a good proportion of the solid wastes at our landfills. If you grow a garden and don't collect food scraps for composting, you are throwing away great organic soil enrichers. Check your library for books that describe the very simple process of composting garbage to create rich humus for your plants. You will experience the great satisfaction of applying potential garbage to useful purposes, and you will save money on commercial fertilizer preparations. The joy of compost is just one more reason to grow a garden!

## Recommended

Brown, Edward Espe, and Deborah Madison. *Greens Cookbook: Extraordinary Vegetarian Cuisine from the Celebrated Restaurant*. New York: Bantam, 1987.

Brown, Edward Espe. *Tassajara Cooking*. Boston: Shambhala, 1986.

Haas, Robert. *Eat to Succeed*. New York: NAL, 1987.

Hausman, Patricia, and Judith B. Hurley. *The Healing Foods: The Ultimate Authority on the Curative Power of Nutrition*. Emmaus, PA: Rodale Press, 1989.

Hynes, H. Patricia. *EarthRight*. Rocklin, CA: Prima, 1990.

Lappé, Frances Moore. *Diet for a Small Planet: 10th Anniversary Edition*. New York: Ballantine, 1985.

Piscatella, Joseph. *Choices for a Healthy Heart*. New York: Workman, 1987.

Robbins, John. *Diet for a New America: How Your Food Choices Affect Your Health, Happiness, and the Future of Life on Earth*. Walpole, NH: Stillpoint, 1987.

Thomas, Anna. *Vegetarian Epicure*. New York: Random House, 1972.

Thomas, Anna. *Vegetarian Epicure: Book 2*. New York: Alfred A. Knopf, 1978.

Toomay, Mindy, and Susann Geiskopf-Hadler. *Fast and Natural Cuisine: A Complete Guide to Easy Vegetarian and Seafood Cooking*. Ashland, OR: Quicksilver Productions, 1983.

# Index

in spicy zucchini noodle
soup with avocado
salsa, 62
in stewed cauliflower and
potato with cumin, 144
in sweet and sour eggplant
sauce, 146
in Tex-Mex tofu and noodles,
198
Cilantro pesto, 34
pasta with, and avocado, 135
Cooking utensils, about, 11–13
Corn
baby, spicy brussels sprouts,
shiitake and, 158
in Mexicali lasagna, 264
in Tex-Mex tofu and noodles,
198
Corn pasta, in pasta salad
Mexicana, 118
Cottage cheese, in spinach and
cheese pesto with
pimiento, 42
Couscous
about, 15
carrot curry soup with, 60
salad with dried-tomato
vinaigrette, 122
salad, creamy, 124
casserole with capers and
tarragon, 270
casserole, curried, 272
Cream sauces. See Dairy-based
stovetop sauces
Cucumber
in couscous salad with
dried-tomato vinai-
grette, 122
in pasta salad with pesto and
peas, 94

sauce, salad in creamy
garlic, 100
Currants, curried pasta salad
with, and almonds, 120
Curry(ied)
carrot soup with couscous, 60
couscous casserole, 272
creamed eggs, 230
pasta salad with currants and
almonds, 120
in spicy cannellini and green
beans with raisins, 244
tomato sauce with peanuts
and tempeh, 206
tomato soup with pasta and
garbanzos, 84

## D

Dairy-based stovetop sauces.
See Contents for list of
recipe titles
recipes, 216–256
tips on, 214–215
Dill, fresh, in sauce of feta,
fresh herbs, and
cashews, 250
Dried mushrooms, about, 8.
See also Porcini
mushrooms, Shiitake
mushrooms
Dried tomato(es). See
Tomato(es), dried

## E

Egg(s)
in basic Alfredo sauce, 226
in couscous casserole with
capers and tarragon, 270
curried creamed, 230

in dried-tomato carbonara,
132
in oregano pesto manicotti,
280
in pasta al pesto frittata, 263
in pasta carbonara senza
carne, 218
in pesto ricotta shells with
herbed tomato sauce,
284
salad with roasted tomatoes,
fresh basil and, 115
in savory mushroom custard
with pasta, 268
in spinach lasagna with port,
288
in summer squash with fresh
basil and Madeira, 154
Eggplant
creamy, and Gorgonzola
sauce, 250
in green tomato sauce with
pasta, 212
in grilled vegetables in
dried-tomato marinade,
152
in hot baba ghanoush with
pasta, 160
in pasta primavera, 192
roasting, 21
sauce, sweet and sour, 146
spicy, salad with calamata
olives, 102
spinach and, with dried
tomatoes and feta, 156
spinach, lasagna, 260
in tempeh and veggies with
miso tahini sauce, 162
Endive, in grilled vegetables
in dried-tomato
marinade, 152

## F

Fats, about, 23
Feta cheese
carrots and artichoke hearts
with pistachios and, 148
in cold pasta with tomatoes,
artichokes, and capers,
112
in dried-tomato pesto with
mint and, 44
in Greek-style pasta salad
with tarragon, 110
lentil, and olive pasta salad,
108
pastina salad with romaine
and, 104
sauce of, fresh herbs, and
cashews, 248
in south of the border pasta,
204
spinach and eggplant with
dried tomato and, 156
tomato and lentil sauce with,
208
Fontina cheese
in brandied mushrooms with
two cheeses, 246
in pizza pasta, 138
Frittata, pasta al pesto, 263

## G

Garbanzo beans
in curried couscous cas-
serole, 272
curried tomato soup with
pasta and, 84
sauce of tomatoes, rosemary
and, 210
in two-bean zuppa, 82
Garlic
about, 4–5, 27

Mustard seeds
  in couscous salad with
      dried-tomato vinai-
      grette, 122
  pasta salad with broccoli
      and, 92

## N
Neufchâtel cheese
  in sauce of mushrooms,
      spinach, and capers for
      tortellini, 274
  in shells filled with dried
      tomatoes and pesto, 286
Nutrition alert, 22–25
Nut(s). *See also* Almonds,
      Cashews, Peanuts,
      Pecans, Pine nuts,
      Walnuts
  about, 8–9
  toasting, 20
Nutmeg
  cream, leeks, carrots and
      pecans in, 216
  ricotta with, and peas, 234

## O
Oil(s)
  calories in, 23
  canola, about, 2
  olive, about, 2
  roasted sesame, about, 2
Olive(s)
  artichokes, pesto, and pasta,
      salad of, 106
  calamata, spicy eggplant
      salad with, 102
  calamata, spicy tomato sauce
      with arugula and, 194
  in dried-tomato carbonara,
      132

in Greek-style pasta salad
      with tarragon, 110
  lentil, feta and pasta salad,
      108
  in pasta oliveto, 182
  in pasta salad Mexicana, 118
  and pimiento pesto, 38
  in pizza pasta, 138
  in spinach lasagna with port,
      288
  in Tex-Mex tofu and noodles,
      198
  in tomato and lentil sauce
      with feta, 208
  in tomato Madeira sauce
      with avocado, 198
  and tomato pesto, 40
Onion(s)
  in garden basket lasagna, 294
  in pasta carbonara senza
      carne, 218
  soup with pasta, French, 68
  tomatoes with sweet
      rosemary, 188
Oregano, fresh
  lemon cream, porcini,
      mustard, and ricotta
      ravioli with, 291
  in sauce of feta, fresh herbs,
      and cashews, 248
  tomato sauce with, 176
Oregano pesto, 36
  manicotti, 280
Oyster mushrooms, with
      cilantro and cream, 220

## P
Parsley
  about, 5
  in cilantro pesto, 34

in oregano pesto manicotti,
280
pesto, shells with herbed
tomato sauce, 284
porcini, mustard and, ravioli
with lemon oregano
cream, 291
in roasted red bell pepper
pesto, 41
sauce, savory, 236
in shells filled with dried
tomatoes and pesto, 286
in spinach eggplant lasagna,
260
in spinach lasagna with port,
288
in spinach nutmeg ravioli
with tomato and brandy
cream, 278
in tofu pesto rollups, 282
Roasting vegetables, 21
Romaine lettuce, pastina salad
with, and feta, 104
Rosemary
and cauliflower soup with
pastina, creamy, 58
in sauce of feta, fresh herbs,
and cashews, 248
sauce of tomatoes, and
garbanzos, 210
tomatoes with sweet,
onions, 188
Rosemary pesto, 33
in acorn squash ravioli with
rosemary walnut sauce,
276
minestrone with, 80

## S

Salads. *See* Contents for list of
recipe titles

recipes, 90–125
tips for, 87–89
Salsa, fresh
recipe for, 172
in south of the border pasta,
204
in Tex-Mex tofu and noodles,
198
Seeding tomatoes, 21
Seeds. *See also* Mustard seeds,
Poppy seed noodles,
Pumpkin seeds,
Sesame seeds, Sun-
flower seeds
about, 8–9
toasting, 20
Sesame butter. *See* Tahini
Sesame seeds
in broccoli, dried tomato,
and ginger cream, 228
in porcini, mustard, and
ricotta ravioli with
lemon oregano cream,
291
in shiitake and spinach pesto
with ginger, 44
in soba in broth with fried
vegetables and *age,* 66
in soba salad with carrots,
snow peas, and sesame
mayo, 116
in spicy brussels sprouts
with baby corn and
shiitake, 158
in sweet and sour eggplant
sauce, 146
toasting, 20
Shells, pasta. *See* Pasta shells
Sherry, about, 3
Shiitake mushrooms
about, 8

pesto rollups, 282
in shells filled with dried
tomatoes and pesto, 286
spicy stir-fried, and green
beans, 140
in spinach eggplant lasagna,
260
in spinach lasagna with port,
288
Tex-Mex, and noodles, 198
Tomato(es), crushed, in
spinach lasagna with
port, 288
Tomato(es), dried
broccoli, and ginger cream,
228
carbonara, 132
in cold pasta in creamy garlic
cucumber sauce, 100
creamy pasta with artichokes
and, 224
in curried couscous cas-
serole, 272
in green tomato sauce with
pasta, 212
in lentil, feta, and olive pasta
salad, 108
marinade, grilled vegetables
in, 152
marinating, 3–4
in Mediterranean asparagus
and artichokes, 150
in oyster mushrooms with
cilantro and cream, 220
pesto with mint, 46
in shells filled with dried
tomatoes and pesto, 286
in spicy cannellini and green
beans with raisins, 244
in spicy zucchini noodle

soup with avocado
salsa, 62
spinach and eggplant with,
and feta, 156
vinaigrette, couscous salad
with, 122
Tomato(es), fresh
angel hair with, and fresh
basil, 180
artichokes, and capers,
salad, 114
in avocado salsa, spicy
zucchini noodle soup
with, 62
blanching and seeding, 20
coulis, quick and simple, 174
in fresh salsa, 172
in light tomato cream with
pesto, 184
Madeira sauce with avocado,
200
pasta with peppers and, 202
in pasta oliveto, 182
in pasta primavera, 192
in pizza pasta, 138
ripening, 3
roasting, 21
sauce of, rosemary and
garbanzos, 210
sauce, herbed, pesto ricotta
shells with, 284
spicy, sauce with arugula
and calamata olives, 194
with sweet rosemary onions,
188
Tomatoes, green, sauce with
pasta, 212
Tomato paste, canned
in black olive and tomato
pesto, 40

316                                                    Index

# More Cookbooks from Prima

Few books have captured the market for health-conscious cooks as the *Lean and Luscious* series has. All three books offer many unique features, including: nutritional breakdowns, comb-binding, and easy-to-prepare recipes that families love.

Over 200 delicious recipes low in both fat and cholesterol, certain to delight any palate. This book includes a wide variety of recipes for soups, barbecues, microwave, stir-fry, and salads.

# To Order Books

Please send me the following items:

| Quantity | Title | Unit Price | Total |
|----------|-------|------------|-------|
| _____ | _____ | $ _____ | $ _____ |
| _____ | _____ | $ _____ | $ _____ |
| _____ | _____ | $ _____ | $ _____ |
| _____ | _____ | $ _____ | $ _____ |
| _____ | _____ | $ _____ | $ _____ |

Shipping and Handling depend on Subtotal.

| Subtotal | Shipping/Handling |
|----------|-------------------|
| $0.00–$14.99 | $3.00 |
| $15.00–$29.99 | $4.00 |
| $30.00–$49.99 | $6.00 |
| $50.00–$99.99 | $10.00 |
| $100.00–$199.99 | $13.50 |
| $200.00+ | Call for Quote |

Foreign and all Priority Request orders:
Call Order Entry department
for price quote at 916/632-4400

This chart represents the total retail price of books only
(before applicable discounts are taken).

Subtotal **$** _____
Deduct 10% when ordering 3-5 books **$** _____
7.25% Sales Tax (CA only) **$** _____
8.25% Sales Tax (TN only) **$** _____
5.0% Sales Tax (MD and IN only) **$** _____
Shipping and Handling* **$** _____
Total Order **$** _____

**By Telephone:** With MC or Visa, call 800-632-8676, 916-632-4400. Mon-Fri, 8:30-4:30
WWW {http://www.primapublishing.com}

**Orders Placed Via Internet E-mail** {sales@primapub.com}
**By Mail:** Just fill out the information below and send with your remittance to

**Prima Publishing**
**P.O. Box 1260BK**
**Rocklin, CA 95677**

My name is _____

I live at _____

City_____ State_____ Zip_____

MC/Visa#_____ Exp. _____

Check/Money Order enclosed for $ _____ Payable to Prima Publishing

Daytime Telephone_____

Signature_____